"The ☉ Manuscript is really beyond words, for reading it is an experience like no other. From the moment I looked upon the cover I could feel the magnitude of this incredible work. For me, reading and integrating Lars Muhl's ☉ Manuscript was not just the reading of a book, but a deep spiritual experience and an initiation of the highest order. This most sacred book has a special place in my home and my heart and I feel it's light still whenever I look upon it. These earthly words will have to suffice to describe something so powerful and indescribable."
Gail Swanson, author of *The Heart of Love : Mary Magdalene Speaks*

"This is an excellent spiritual book. Not just because it goes into the depths of the heart and to the essence of spirituality, but also because page after page is adorned with brilliant spiritual experiences. Furthermore, the development of the storyline and the poetic language are of such high standard that these qualities alone make the book worth recommending."
Lars Harrekilde, *Nyt Aspekt*

"A remarkable testimonial from the world of the mystics, experienced by a present day mystic. One of our time's experience-religious classics; a totally unusual book that offers a peek into a part of the mind that others are too shy to talk about. A rare glimpse into the mystical universe."
Anders Laugesen, *Kristeligt Dagblad*

"The ☉ Manuscript opens up to the very centre of man's true mystery. . . . [It] not just another spiritual sweetener, but the beginning of a most exciting journey for anyone who reads it. The books are not to be read merely to be 'understood', but to be absorbed into the very texture of your conscious being and your higher Self."
Kirsten Puggaard, publisher, Lemuel Books

About the Author

Lars Muhl was born in Aarhus in 1950. He attended The Royal Academy of Music, Aarhus (Det Jyske Musikkonservatorium) from 1974 to 1976. For many years, he was a successful singer-songwriter – first as a band member, and then from 1986 as a solo artist. In 1996, he was awarded the WCM's Songwriters Million Certificate.

The author has had a great interest in spirituality from a very young age, and, concurrently with his music, he studied the world's religions and esoteric knowledge. Then in 1996, he was struck down by an unexplained illness, which neither doctors nor alternative therapists could diagnose. This was the start of a completely new existence and the beginning of that quest he has so grippingly described in *The Seer*. In 1999 Lars Muhl decided to leave music to concentrate fully on his spiritual interests.

Lars Muhl is now working as a healer, lecturer and writer, specialising in spirituality and alternative treatments. In 2003 he started Hearts and Hands, a non-profit and apolitical aid organization based on the voluntary work of various therapists. The aim is to help people who are suffering from life crises such as cancer and stress-related illnesses. In 2009 Lars Muhl and his wife Githa Ben-David founded Gilalai Institute for Energy and Consciousness.

To the memory of Calle Montségur (1934–2007)

◇◇◇◇◇◇◇◇◇◇◇◇◇◇◇◇◇

LARS MUHL

The

SCANDINAVIAN
BESTSELLER

VOLUME I OF 'THE O MANUSCRIPT'

WATKINS PUBLISHING
LONDON

Those who dance are often condemned
by those who cannot hear the music

I

It was an ice-cold day in February. The kind of day where the Copenhagen Central Station is anything but inviting. I dragged my suitcases up the stairs to get out of the chilling wind from the platform and quite deliberately ignored the beggars and the down-and-outs squatting on old newspapers and waving their blue coffee-pots at the passers-by. My own budget was more than over the limit, and, furthermore, I felt dizzy. I felt nauseated. I wasn't myself at all. Had I misunderstood something, since I lost my balance to such a frightening degree? And then just now, when I was about to embark on what was probably the most important journey of my life.

I drank a bottle of club soda at the cafeteria and found a corner where I could sit relatively undisturbed in order to recover. I had a couple of hours before the night train for Cologne was scheduled to depart. In spite of how far I thought I had come, I still sat there and felt like a totally abandoned novice. Unsuccessfully, I had tried to sell the account of my journey to a major newspaper just two days earlier. But how were they to know that a train journey to southern Spain could be more exotic in this day and age, than an aeroplane trip to the Antarctic Continent, simply because it takes longer? They knew better at the DSB travel agency. It was the first trip of this kind that they had sold for several years.

'Are you sure?' the woman asked wonderingly and slightly curious as I booked the ticket.

I chose not to start a major explanation about my having stopped flying many years ago, but couldn't help smiling at the paradox that I was about to begin a 48-hour train journey to Spain, in principle, in order to fly. Well, not by plane, but still ...

The characteristic greasy smell of today's special: meat, cabbage, gravy and potatoes, mixed with too much smoke and nicotine, made my stomach turn and I had to concentrate in order not to be sick. I was cold in spite of the heat, had sweat on my forehead, and I shivered so much that I had to hold on to the bottle with both hands. I drank some soda and tried to think about something else.

'But isn't this Lars Muhl?' A far too optimistic voice cut through the noise from the plates and cutlery. I looked up and nodded automatically. A man handed me a paper napkin and a pen: 'Could I please have your autograph?'

He smiled at the girl standing next to him, who seemed to be his daughter. I was just about to be sick. Beads of sweat trailed down my face as I grabbed the pen and wrote my name while getting up from my seat. I then ran as fast as I could towards the men's room.

When I got back, the man and his daughter had

disappeared. It was the first autograph I had written for ages. A middle-aged woman who was hanging on to a strong beer at the neighbouring table scowled disapprovingly at me through a black eye and I could almost hear her thinking: 'Who the hell do you think you are?' Well, I would really like to know that myself. I closed my eyes and tried to concentrate on the present situation. But somehow, my thoughts automatically went back. Back to the day when my career as a singer categorically ended, and my present journey started. Back to all that went before the NOW.

I had always known that a person is more than his or her mere personality. I had always known that the real person is to be found somewhere behind all the defences and the protective shields of titles, careers and jobs. I had always been aware that no matter how well known, how rich and how celebrated you are, there aren't enough fans, money and attention in the world to close the gap and ease the pain which all the hullabaloo carries with it. I have always known that notwithstanding your living conditions and social position, ultimately, all this seems strangely illusory, seen in the perspective of eternity.

Since childhood I have been familiar with another reality. From my 10th to my 12th year, each evening before I fell asleep, I had some unfamiliar and painful kundalini experiences, with the result that I hardly slept at all during this period. Since I wasn't able to share these experiences with anyone I became more and more introvert and unable to function. I found social situations difficult to handle and did badly at school. However, this didn't stop me reading on my own. When I was 15 years old I received the sufi-mystic Hazrat Inayat Khan's book *Gayan, Vadan, Nirtan* by mail. I don't know who sent it. But the book was a revelation and inspired me to read other books by Khan. The problem was, however, that what I read and studied all somehow connected to my knowledge of the other reality and thus stood out in sharp contrast to all my school learning. When finally I left the school in 1966 to throw myself into the intensity of life as a musician, I was hoping that this, once and for all, would cut out the reality which had made me so damned lonely and which no one else seemed to care about.

My attempt seemed to succeed, when destiny brought the band I was playing in to Israel in 1969, where we were supposed to tour for a couple of months. We played for the soldiers at the army summer camps, for the students at the universities and for the young people at the clubs and the discotheques. Drugs were more or less compulsory but unfortunately also banned in Israel at the time. Thus, when we were arrested with cannabis and amphetamine during a raid at the hotel, we were forced to spend about a week at the notorious remand prison in Jaffa just outside of Tel Aviv. It thus took a stone bench to sleep on, a cold water faucet to wash by, a hole in the middle of the cell for the necessary relief and a very primitive form of communication between prisoners and guards, to wake me from my magic sleep.

During one of the exercise rounds one of my fellow prisoners showed me the holes in the ground measuring two by two metres, where they kept the insane, the murderers and the rapists, each in his hole with an iron grid over his head: in the daytime a burning oven, at night an icy refrigerator. Each time a prisoner passed by and spat or threw a rock at the miserable creatures, they reacted with inarticulate and hysterical howls and an infernal noise from the shackles, which they banged against the iron grids. It was hard to accept, that almost at the same time the American astronaut Armstrong put his foot on the moon with the words: 'One small step for man – one giant leap for mankind.' I for one didn't understand it. What did it mean? Was this a cosmic joke or a part of civilized man's catering to the ultimate duality dividing life into black and white, heaven and hell.

It was as if everything that happened during the three months in Israel simply sharpened my psychic senses, which up and until that time I had frantically tried to hide. Whether it was due to the ancient, historical surroundings with all their myths and religious traditions, I do not know; however, I nevertheless started getting sporadic visions from ancient times and heard voices from a strange and yet familiar world. Furthermore, for the first time in my life I also met another person with the same experiences. Simon. A Jewish boy, 13 years old, who also knew about this other reality.

One day, sitting on our terrace facing the street, he happened to pass by. Even seeing him at a distance as he was approaching I immediately knew who he was. Having reached the terrace he stopped. He also recognized me. I invited him in for tea and from that day on we met almost daily. One day he gave me a necklace with a piece of jewelry on which he had done some filigree work. A round globe with a piece of cedar wood inside it and a spiral-shaped cone fastened to it. The globe symbolized the earth. The little piece of cedar wood symbolized King Solomon's Ginkgo Maidenhair Tree, the Cosmic Tree, which possessed a magical power. The spiral symbolized the eternal death and rebirth, and the transformation of matter to spirit. As I put it on, a large, affirmative YES sounded through me and it felt like a blessing.

Meeting Simon, combined with the psychic experiences, made me believe that I had now found the place where I belonged and in my euphoria I forgot the realities of my life. Maybe there is some truth in the saying that a chain is never stronger than its weakest link since one day I found that the necklace with the piece of jewelry was gone. It was like a bad omen. And yet another awakening. This time an awakening to the unavoidable fact that it was time to go home. Immediately prior to my departure I had my first out-of-body experience.

Now, more than 30 years later, I was sitting at the Copenhagen Central Station feeling out of the body in a different way; well, more like out of place. What had summoned me here? Was it time – my time – which finally was about to reach its point of eternity, where ends meet and two realities become one?

Each life is a journey and mine was no exception. But had I come to a cul-de-sac or was the journey almost over? Seen from the point of view of the traditional idea of what constitutes a good life, mine seemed in many ways to be a failure. For more than 30 years I had been fighting a losing battle with a career as a musician and later as a singer. I had had decent results, but each time it got really serious something in me pulled in the opposite direction. Away from the public eye and the superficial promotion and duties. As time went by, this something seemed to take over more and more of my reality.

Here I was watching it all from a distance. Watching the lie with which I had betrayed myself and which had kept me in a condition that finally had become unbearable, simply because it made me ill. For too long did I believe that it was possible to walk in two opposite directions. To be part of the music scene with all that it entailed and at the same time to live quietly in contemplation as some kind of mystic. To relate to a static, unified, strictly intellectual and materially focused world while at the same time I was really rediscovering and getting to know the other hidden and totally different reality – it simply wasn't possible. Finding myself on stage in the big tent at the Roskilde Festival in 1991 the question suddenly struck me in the middle of a song: 'What are you doing here?' I could suddenly see myself from outside of myself, I could hear myself talking to the audience, trying to regain my composure with a lame, 'hey, hey, hey' and to get in contact with the reality of the festival, which was slowly disappearing in a fog of beer and senseless drunkenness. It was totally surreal and of course impossible, since you cannot get out of the boat once it is launched. That same evening I decided to end the tour, and that same year I left my home town and moved to a small island.

'The train for Cologne with an estimated departure of 6.45 p.m. will arrive at platform 3 in about 30 minutes,' a metallic voice proclaimed through the loudspeakers.

I checked the time on my own wristwatch. I myself felt like an island in the middle of the steaming sea of people dining at the cafeteria. The place was filling up. I bought yet another club soda. The nausea and the dizziness were disappearing. In the arrival hall the beggars sat freezing and shaking on the benches trying to keep warm. The passers-by didn't notice them at all. All in all it didn't seem as if anyone noticed anything. Buttoned up, eyes ahead. Apparently, all were sufficient to themselves. What were they thinking? Where were they going? What about me? Wasn't I sufficient to myself? Had my ability to partake in social activities improved since I withdrew to the island? Hardly! But I did it because I had to.

Had I not frequently heard people expressing their wishes to be sufficiently wealthy to be able to retire to a rural idyll in order to focus on themselves. But it wasn't like that at all. I was not wealthy. On the contrary. The material renunciation caused by the collapse in my career would have given most citizens in a welfare state nightmares. The process I had been through was a paradoxical mixture of an existential stripping down and a mental breakdown.

Having settled down on the island I started writing as a natural part of the process of tidying-up. Slowly I began to realize that language constituted an important part of my change and after the publication of my first book, more followed. My fascination by the first Taoist and Buddhist writings turned into further extensive, comparative studies of religion, the Christian mystics, Sufism, various occult and Christian heresy schools. Lately I had started studying Aramaic on my own, the language that Yeshua (Jesus) is supposed to have spoken. A daily practice of various forms of quietude and meditation only distanced me further from my former life. But something or other in me kept me vainly clinging to a small, final and stubborn part of what was left of my diversified show biz career.

Until the day when circumstances helped me make the decision that I myself had hesitated making. During the recording for *Mandolina*, which would turn out to be my last album, the record company suddenly informed me that after fusing with a multinational company they had decided to cease our business relationship (before it really started) for reasons unknown to me. This meant that the contract we had just signed and which included yet another album, was now cancelled. Only reluctantly did the company accept that I could finish what I was in the middle of doing. A lot of work, if not directly wasted, was certainly published in an unfinished condition. It was very frustrating in every way.

The recording companies didn't treat me kindly any more. The commercial expectations for my songs had not paid off and from one day to the other I had no access to my income.

Was it all an element of the irony of fate or was it the efforts of a growing commercialization of the industry trying to clean the recording trade of the last alien substances? I couldn't help thinking about a conversation I once overheard between two managing directors of recording companies, one of whom dryly remarked, that apart from having to work with the artists, the music business wasn't bad at all.

It seemed as if an extensive part of my life was over. It just happened. Like snapping my fingers. It was not until later, that I understood that you are not easily forgiven when you move out of the limelight, when most artists feel that, more or less, it is this limelight that is giving them their livelihood. However, my problem was that I didn't belong there. From then on, my downhill drive went faster and faster. The intervals between phone calls widened and finally the phone didn't ring at all. When I found out that I also didn't have anyone to call, I pulled the plug and cancelled my phone subscription. I was where I wanted to be. Wasn't this what I wanted? Also, when apparently my economic situation went from the acceptable to the more than strained, maybe, finally, I had reached the point of no return. Perhaps I had started to realize that it was time to take care of my real self. Was I finally beginning to understand that life is too short for mere trivialities?

'The train for Cologne will arrive at platform 3 in a few minutes.'

Bending over to lift my suitcases, I felt dizzy. But while crossing the arrival hall I sensed a slight electric current running through my spine. It felt like a very fragile current slowly spreading its energy through my whole body, removing any sign of dizziness. I flicked a coin of 20 kroner into a coffee pot and went down to the platform and the waiting train.

2

I placed my suitcase on the upper shelf. It was covered by a worn, woollen blanket and a sheet, which smelt powerfully of an indefinable but very strong disinfectant.

Travelling on a second class sleeper is only for those who travel light. All dimensions are created from a diminutive and ascetic picture of the world. The size of the berth, washing facilities and lavatory indicate that travelling is just a short phase, a discreet intermezzo, emphasized yet again by the long series of arrivals and departures, hellos and good-byes, absences and expectations, kisses and hugs, tears and sadness, which you witness along the way and which mark out the ephemeral station of any train journey and any life. Paradoxically it is also proof that man and his life is more than just a haphazard complex of unstable qualities and unpredictable influences.

Life is an expression of unity no matter how fragmented

it may seem to be. It had taken me many years to realize that. It was not until my own life felt reduced and limited that I needed more space. It was not until I had lost all that I thought was important and impossible to live without, in fact everything that makes life complicated and impossible – not until then did I begin to have an inkling of how magnificent and unlimited life can be in all its simplicity. But such recognition was not painless.

Hinting at the possibility of another, more open and much freer reality – that for example a musical note could be shaped like a pyramid and that forgiveness could happen faster than the speed of light – was asking to be burned at the stake of an anaesthetized time of roaring silence and patronizing sarcasm. I am telling you!

The sleeper was full as the train grindingly started to roll. A businessman on the opposite berth, wearing blue-and-white striped pyjamas, completed his evening toilet with great difficulty and according to a meticulously planned ritual. Below him a stout German was wrestling his equally stout luggage and on the lower berth two young men from Copenhagen were exchanging canned beer and bad jokes, while an elderly gentleman in the berth below my own was snoring loudly. I slowly let go and allowed myself to float into the clear, frosty and starry night, over the sleepers and into unknown tunnels and the black holes of foreign universes, back to the year where I found myself stuck in the furthest corner of the maze, the shabby cul-de-sac of my own life.

It was the year when I fell into the dark night of the soul. It happened through a series of attacks, which physically meant that the back of my neck hurt like hell, I felt nauseated, lost all energy and had to stay in bed for days on end. It was like being caught in a no-mans-land between the conscious and the unconscious, between being awake and asleep, the feeling of iron. To be locked into an almost hermetically sealed torture chamber, where everything was heavy and slow and blown apart. Every thought disappeared in a lethargic stupor almost before it was begun. The thought of having to reach for a glass of water seemed such an insurmountable obstacle that I usually gave it up. Once in a while when I came to, I managed to think that this must be hell before sinking back into bottomless darkness. I had only experienced something similar in 1962, when I started my first book, which was written in a trance-like state similar to this one.

For two months I stayed in the same room, living on coffee and aspirin, clacking away at my old typewriter or lying unconscious on my equally old couch. Night and day disappeared in a monotonous fog and only my writing changed it into something like euphoria; an unreal, psychosomatic condition which didn't stop until I had written the last dot in the book.

Now the condition came back and made me unfit for work for longer and longer periods of time. A number of visits to the doctor, examinations at the hospital and at several specialists and alternative healers had no effect at all. At one time I was almost unconscious in my bed for about two weeks without getting anything to eat and drink but biscuits and water. They didn't even manage to find the reason for my condition when one day I fainted at my neighbour's house and had to spend the rest of the day in hospital supported by oxygen and a drip. As time went by I experienced more and more that I had to let go of the music since it had given way to this other thing. My crisis was total. After more than two years like this I didn't want to live anymore.

And then it happened – the unavoidable. It happens at least once in every man's life, although you may not notice it. The condition you are in is such that all too easily you disappear into the no-man's-land of pain and self-centredness, where all is lost and immovable. But the time was ripe because I was ripe, since I didn't have any other way out and nowhere to go. Was it a sign or was it an angel? In my case it was the latter. The angel came in the shape of a colleague from the slowly growing but still very small and invisible family. She gave me the telephone number that was going to turn everything upside down.

'Call the Seer and let him help you,' she said before disappearing into thin air. I just stood there, alternately staring into the hole in the air left by the angel and at the note she had pressed into my hand. 'Only between 8 and 9 a.m.' it said in the parentheses following the phone number.

The Seer?

That evening I took a long walk along Frederiksberg Allé before going to bed in my room at Weber's Hotel, totally exhausted.

During the night I had a dream. In it I am walking down a long, deserted road. It ends abruptly and I'm standing at the edge of a precipice looking out into the universe. The quiet is underlined by an almost inaudible but very beautiful, deep and continuous note. The sound of matter. The sound that holds everything together. Touching and unutterable. I hear myself speaking in Aramaic: *Nehwey sibyanak aykana d'shmaya aph b'arab.* I remember. *Thy will be done on earth as it is in Heaven.* I now understand what these words really mean. *Let that happen on earth which is written between the stars. Unfold the light of the universe through each and everyone of us according to the laws of the universe.*

It was half past eight when I woke up. Again this dull feeling of iron at the edges of my consciousness. It took some time before I remembered what had happened the day before. Then I remembered the dream, the angel and the phone number. I got up feeling quite dizzy and started going through the pockets of my jacket and trousers. No such luck. Panic. It was as if already I had realized what I was about to lose if I let this slip through my fingers. Finally. The slip of paper was in the breast pocket of my shirt. I dialled the number and held my breath. I waited and waited. I could follow the slow shift from the hotel telephone system to the phone company's by the sound of the series of changing notes. I was just about to hang up when I was finally connected, just to hear that the number was engaged. A lifetime of butterflies in my stomach. Looked at my watch. Almost nine, waited and tried again.

Still busy. Ten past nine, connection. I sat thinking that my telephone call was making a sound in the house of an unknown person, and that at the end of this ring tone that person had decided not to answer my call. I let it ring for a while and hung up.

Back at the island my condition improved and I found my usual rhythm alternating between my work with the Aramaic, which by now had really caught my attention, and periods of dizziness. Several times I was tempted to call the number again but for some reason or other I postponed it.

Getting further and further into the Aramaic language a totally new world opened to me. As early as 1989 Dr Edith R Stauffer from Psycho Synthesis International had sent me a copy of an Aramaic excerpt from The New Testament, *The Khaboris Manuscript*. This made it clear that the Aramaic is able to express the transpersonal psychology to such a degree, that the syntax at the same time can describe the correlation between thought, acknowledgement, perception, reason, the ability to dream, the structure of mind, understanding, human attitudes and behaviour. It does not distinguish between the mental, the physical, the emotional and the spiritual. Between cause and effect. This means that each word and each idea is totally neutral in its root, but that it is activated through the suffixes '-ta' or '-oota'. To me this was a revolutionary discovery, which suddenly gave the words of Yeshua a new and deeper power and meaning than I got from the Greek translation of The New Testament. And slowly it dawned on me, that not only the meaning of the words but also the sound of them have an effect on the physical as well as on the spiritual level.

At that time I had no idea how much these studies would mean later on.

During this period, when I was mainly studying Leshana Aramaya, I had a fit one morning, which was so severe that I could hardly get out of bed. But I knew that it was now or never. The small slip of paper with the phone number was attached to the wall of my study with a pin. All my reservations and all the butterflies were gone as I lifted the receiver and dialled the number.

'Yes,' an articulate and neutral voice replied.

I introduced myself.

'What can I do for you?' the voice continued.

'I'd like to make an appointment,' I replied.

'Well, it'll be another six months before I can fit you in. What is your problem?'

I explained my condition as well as I could.

'Just a moment, I'll see what I can do.'

It sounded as if he had put the receiver down. I listened to the sound of silence in the room at the other end of this connection; a kind of soft, white noise which seemed to continue indefinitely. I don't know for how long I sat like this but suddenly the voice was back:

'You'll be okay until we meet again.'

He gave me the address and hung up.

I sat for a long time with the receiver in my hand, completely overwhelmed, before I could replace it. My thoughts wandered across the fields outside my window. I was suddenly struck as

The Night
(Mask made by Anne Maria Galmez, 1989 – Photo: Jan Jul)

if by a hammer and I knew I had to get back to bed before I fainted. I just managed to think that the Seer was just another quack before sliding down into a deep, dreamless sleep.

'Cologne in half an hour,' a voice boomed in the corridor.

I opened my eyes. On the shelf opposite me I only saw the businessman's well organized luggage. A heavy cloud of aftershave and toothpaste told me that he had been up for quite a while. I looked at my watch. It was half past six. The elderly gentleman, who had been snoring loudly during the night, was also up. The German must have got out in Hamburg, since he and all his luggage were gone. The two young people from Copenhagen were still sleeping heavily. I dressed lying down, and put my shoes on. The businessman was in the corridor, well groomed and smoking a cigar. There was a queue at the bathroom door. When it was finally my turn, I decided not to use it when I saw the condition it was in. Someone had plugged the toilet bowl with toilet paper and then apparently had shit in the sink. The floor was a lake of urine and the stench was unbelievable. The shower wasn't much better. I packed my bags and stood watching the lively activity and couldn't help thinking which one of all those nice people was so self-centred that he literally didn't give a shit about other people.

Cologne Central Station was, if possible, even more cold and inhospitable than the Central Station in Copenhagen. There was heavy traffic everywhere. People in all degrees of sleepiness were on their way to work. I just had time for a quick visit to the bathroom and a cup of coffee before catching the train for Paris. I sat down at a table in an espresso bar and wondered why we are so busy that we don't notice what is going on around us. In 50 years all these people would be gone or be in nursing homes thinking back over their busy lives, while the train station would be just as filled with people, the only difference being, that it would be other busy people. And when they were gone, others would follow. The stage set would outlive the actors. The extras and the stars in an everlasting staff turnover, one team after the other. Forward, forward, don't look up, never look back, as if no one dared to stop, fearing that they might lose face and perhaps end up as the homeless in the corner or the beggar on his bench. Perhaps it was better to cling to the illusion of eternal material comfort, forgetting all until that one day, when we all have to leave. An eternal escape from the hour of truth.

Was it this hour that had finally caught up with me? The day when I thought I had called just another quack. If someone had told me that I was going to die during my sleep, I would certainly have accepted this as a sensible solution. But this was not to be. After half an hour's sleep I woke up to a new world. Immediately I felt that all had changed but could hardly believe it. Did I really wake up to a new life? Was the more than two years of nightmare really over?

For the first time I felt close to something peaceful. But although the pain was gone I had not forgotten it. On the other hand, I probably had a deeper sense of gratitude. My thoughts kept returning to the voice on the phone. It had easily pierced my armour, opening up a painful spot in me which far too long had been locked. After this miraculous improvement of my condition, this spot now lay open and vulnerable, waiting for my own awakening that I might heal the wound. I saw the beauty and the ugliness of the pain. I saw that it was as much beast as it was human. I saw that I could pet it the way you might pet a cat. The nature of pain is as ruthless as a cat seems to be, when it plays with a mouse just before it kills it. But just as it is impossible for an animal to be evil, since it is just following its natural instincts, pain will follow its laws until people understand that these laws are not static but flexible, and that the one suffering from it may heal and transform. As early as the year 630 John Climacus wrote: 'A man having received the sentence of death is not concerned with the repertoire of the theatre.'

I began to understand the role that pain had played in my life. I began to understand how, at another level than the level of reason, it had opened my eyes to the suffering of others. I began to understand that any kind of pain is a tool in the hands of a higher cause, since in the long run it undermines any kind of judgement and any kind of half-heartedness, in fact, that it quite literally cuts to the bone. In the most effective way it transforms self-pity and selfishness to compassion and attention. Seeing and understanding this with both my body and soul wasn't possible before the pain had disappeared, and it was all due to a person that I did not know and had never met.

There were some distinctive patterns in me that started to dissolve. During all the time I had lived on the island I had started to experience the external appearances such as nature, the forest, the sea and the elements, more intensely, which opened my eyes to the same nature – the elements – within myself. I didn't see another person for long periods of time. Not that I wanted to isolate myself or to be without the company of others, but because it was necessary to find my way into that which for far too long had been hiding behind a career in the limelight. I had experienced a new kind of simplicity, which at times could be so intense that I felt as if I was disappearing. I started to practise focusing my thoughts. I practised controlling them, ignoring them or letting them have their way. It was almost frighteningly easy to give in to the temptation of letting go. Just to leave everything and disappear into silence. It was a condition that didn't make it any easier for me to function. On the other hand, I also knew that there was no going back. Although in some ways alarming, I felt that the underlying gratitude became a deeply felt reality to a degree that I had always known existed, and which now gave me a new kind of openness. It was neither particularly melancholy nor melodramatic. It just happened. Like that. Like an old summer bee buzzing around in a window in slow motion knowing that it was soon going to die. It was not that it couldn't get through the glass. But why should it? It could see everything through the window pane. I was not a bee, but a part of me knew about the cycle of bees. It happened one day as I was walking into the forest. I suddenly hovered across a clearing and found a treetop. I just sat there and fell out of time. Into the universe. Into the centre. I saw how beautiful life can be. Without any commotion, without any filters. But I soon sensed that I shouldn't stay in that openness too long. Not as a human being. Because you might forget your purpose and get lost, so that you wouldn't be able to find your way back.

Sitting in the treetop not thinking at all, it was as if I were in an inner room. There must have been an opening in it since a mild and warm light shone in. The appearing shadows turned into an understanding and were no longer an obstacle. I sat quite still. No effort. No wishes. I felt the walls dissolve and disappear. As if a veil had been drawn away. Everything happened in one single movement. Nothing else existed. I was in the middle of it, was part of it as a slight shivering. I slowly opened my arms. From above, the light fell over me like glittering rain filling me with something. Beyond words. Silence is a part of truth. The only word that might cover it is the word 'certainty'. I sank into certainty, where everything is united and where we come from and are at home. There was no *inside* and no *outside*, no *I want to* or *I shall*, just this quiet certainty. At a distance I saw my old spent self, hanging on a cross-like tree. No pain. Not pathetic. No guilt. No sin. No shame. All was in unity. In light. Here! At the same moment I was aware that right now an old summer bee was dying on my windowsill. I slid down from the tree. I could see everything. Life flowed unimpeded through me. I came round in the forest. Tears flowing freely.

So this was freedom. I had now seen it. Been in it. Although a glimpse only. I was ecstatic, although in a strange, quiet way, in spite of my pounding heart. I was not for a moment in any doubt that I had been at the centre of my being, totally devoid of the endless series of big and small needs that normally make us blind.

After a few days of peace I suddenly got disorientated and this soon turned into sadness. Concurrent with tangible reality moving closer, the deep abyss between the two states became painfully clear and it was hard to see how they could ever be united.

It was during this period that the last sliver of interest in the superficial circus of show business disappeared. I simply didn't have the strength anymore to relate to it. It had been like this for a long time, but not until now did I understand it in a physical sense. The many years in solitude on the island, without newspaper, radio and television, had made it easier for me to relate to the basics of life. It was much easier to get rid of all the masks. It was now easier to see that the pure and the vulnerable in me, which I wrongly had thought were mistakes or weaknesses not to be seen, in reality were the only true prerequisites for my existence. Having lived outdoors for a long time had robbed me of all the escape routes that normally occupy man. I knew from my own life that far too often I partook in the endless and nervous chase for surrogates to sweeten my life and to keep me from looking at it. We had always been told that the pain would cease if quite literally we would move away from the spot where we were at a specific time. That the party was somewhere else. This attitude, more or less, was the birthplace of the whole social structure of the Western world. On the basis of this it had been possible to maintain the illusion that it was morally acceptable to continue an unlimited growth and an overproduction of unnecessary goods and deadening entertainment. And I understood that even the apparently meaningful illusions still, and maybe even first and foremost, were considered to be entertainment. That even though it may make the illusion more acceptable, it was just another self-increasing alibi.

I was of course very much aware that I wasn't the first person to realize this. I knew that I had to get through the crises, which arose when the rug is pulled away from under our old life patterns. If I wasn't supposed to live by my music, what then? If I no longer was a singer, what was I then? It was frightening, suddenly being without an income. It was frightening not knowing how to find money for the next rent. It was the more frightening since it became absolutely clear how important this kind of security had been in my life. That the fear of losing the little I had, all the time had been lurking in the wings like an invisible force, which had run my life. It was the year that I took the decision to completely let go. It was the year where the album appeared that would mark the end of my career. The sinking feeling in my stomach – the great hole in my heart.

On the day the album was released, I went to the beach to watch the announced eclipse of the sun and had the very extraordinary experience of seeing that all the rocks as far as I could see, big and small, were standing upright as if pointing to the sun. A sign? Perhaps a sign that the night was almost over.

I ran as fast as I could. The voice from the loudspeaker had just announced that the train for Paris would be leaving in a few minutes. I heaved my suitcase through the door and managed to jump on board the moment the wheels started turning.

3

Within half a year the last of the remains disintegrated. The claustrophobic condition which had been a firm part of the old world, was now replaced by the open and edifying air sickness, which attacks you when you stand at the edge of an old abyss looking into the universe, very much aware that within a minute or so you will take that step forward and disappear into the blue. The six months seemed like an eternity. Never had I been so poor and felt so rich. Once in a while the past still caught up with me and I had to take a major roller-coaster trip. An agreement about writing a musical was cancelled without warning and it began to look like more than a coincidence that what seemed to be my last door to the music business was slammed shut with a bang. At the same time I received a letter from the newspaper for which, off and on, I reviewed literature. They regretted to inform me that they no longer needed my services. I felt *persona non grata* in every possible way. During these periods it was still difficult to realize and accept that my time as a singer was over and that it would never come back, since my work with music had somehow always been an illusion. I now had to realize that I could not let myself be lured into believing the same thing about being a writer, just because a few of my manuscripts had been published. And this was what could still hurt so terribly much: to realize that I was nothing, and even worse, to accept that I would never be anything – I would just be.

Soon, however, it became very clear that *to be* wasn't something I could just practise, this was something I had to learn. My neurotic fear of the abyss was now mixed with a fascination for it. I cautiously moved close to the edge. It started to dawn on me. Everything I thought had been a conspiracy against me I now saw was just a mirage created by my own projections. I had split a whole universe into bits and pieces by letting them grow. For the sake of my own convenience I had placed all my own defects in others. The defects that I quite self-righteously refused to see in myself. I now had to learn to function in the empty space that was left. It was during this process I understood, that in spite of all our rules and systems and intentions of peace and tolerance, we usually only managed to produce chaos, noise and pollution. We arrive in this world screaming noisily, we walk through it, just to leave a boundless mess behind as we leave it again.

It was an art form to let go. Each day had its challenging renunciations. One veil after the other lifted, and along with them the most persistent of my prejudices. One by one I left my mistaken beliefs behind, which had held me in a vice most of my life. I even had to let go of the sadness and the shame. When finally the day came that I had waited for, there wasn't much left of the one I once thought was me. The day of the appointed consultation with The Seer.

A misty rain fell as I walked along Store Kongensgade. I walked in a daze. And still I remember everything. A couple wearing matching sailor shoes and pulling their bikes. A mother with a red pram; her parchment-like transparency and the heartbreaking cries from the child. Two policemen crossing the road, one of them looking as if he had been crying. An old man entering a bus at a bus stop, his curved hand full of wisdom and death. A girl on a green bicycle in the opposite direction; burning eyes and the well-shaped posterior in a pair of jeans on a saddle. A green messenger. A taxi which had just rammed into the rear end of a car; broken glass from a tail light and angry voices and hysteria too long repressed. A woman's mysterious smile and lazy walk; maybe because she had just left her lover's bed. A green door in the house opposite from the police station; the dryness of my mouth.

I opened the door and stepped into a stairway that still smelled of the past like a luxurious home for a well-to-do family. From far above I heard the sound of shuffling feet going upwards. I followed. A door opened and closed again and for a short moment I heard voices speaking in a foreign tongue. There were echoes of my own feet. On a landing a stubborn cactus in a pot with dried-out soil. I rang the bell at the floor above and looked through the black square on the door, where the name sign had been. From somewhere in the building I heard the sound of a toilet being flushed and some blurred voices disappear into the maze of muffled sounds running into the river of noise from the cars in the street. I pressed the doorbell again. I heard it ringing in a room somewhere in the apartment. No reaction. I looked at the note again: '2nd left'. I looked at my watch. Two minutes to three. I waited. Tried again. Not a sound. Five minutes past three. The front door slammed shut down below. Light steps were on their way up. They got closer. I turned around and looked into a pair of black eyes. She handed me an envelope. I took it and was about to say something, but her shoes danced a flamenco on her way down at top speed. I looked at the envelope. My name was on it. I then followed the flamenco dancer. As I got to the street I just managed to see the posterior in jeans getting on to the green saddle and disappear in the traffic. Behind me I heard the lock of the door clicking shut. A cold wind blew around the corner and pushed at the heavy smell of diesel. I opened the envelope and took out a sheet of paper, 'Libraire 'Le Galois' Montségur-Village N 19, September 30th, 7 a.m'. was the laconic message. It was signed, 'Crede Et Vicisti – C de M'.

It had stopped raining. Across the city roofs the sun was disappearing behind a black cloud. A well-known critic with dark rings under his eyes was eating a bun outside a baker's shop. On the other side of the street a mother was scolding her child, who was happily jumping up and down in a puddle. Behind the windows in an apartment a poet might at this moment be writing a poem about it all. *Crede et Vicisti!* Believe and win! I walked towards Kongens Nytorv.

The train was filled with businessmen in Hugo Boss suits, sitting with laptop offices on their knees and talking on cell phones. They looked like a painting by Magritte. I had obtained a window seat and looked out on a bleak landscape dotted over with equally dismal villages. A row of colourless, artificial pearls on strings of power lines strung between whole forests of electricity pylons which became more and more chaotic and impenetrable the closer we got to Brussels. I couldn't help thinking that these power lines somehow symbolized the financial and political energies merging here to become a river of capsized expectations, stranded in over-administration and bureaucracy, just like Brussels itself looked like a suburb of a metropolis that did not exist at all. A pipedream? A dream? A nightmare?

There was a nervous and hectic energy in the carriage, where cell phones produced the same digital waltzes and marches in endless monotony. Some of the Magritte-men had been exchanged with other Magritte-men who did their best to look just as important as their predecessors. This was a reality where no wobbling about was tolerated. Brussels Central Station seemed as neat and cleansed of social riffraff as the European conscience had to be full of glittering repressions. As the train rattled through the forest of power poles, destination Paris, it was a reminder that the vision of economic security that was constantly thrown at us, in reality is identical with the lie that only creates losers and sick people.

Standing at Kongens Nytorv, the note from the Seer in hand, I decided to take the decisive step toward the abyss. Well, I really told myself that I could hear his voice calling me to the edge. Based on the motto that the one who has nothing, also has nothing to lose, I spent the following months preparing for my journey.

I knew a little about Montségur beforehand. I knew that it was a small town and a mountain with a fortress, situated in the French part of the Pyrenees. I knew the tale about the southern French heretics, the Cathars, the *bons hommes*, and their fateful deaths on the Inquisition stakes at the foot of Montségur as a culmination of the Albigensian Crusade in the year 1244.

The Cathars considered themselves to be the true Christians. Part of their learning rested on primitive Christian, Gnostic, Jewish and Islamic ideas, which at all decisive points differed from the Roman Church. The daily bread was for the Cathars the spiritual bread, and both women and men could become priests, *perfecti*, in their community. The

Cathar movement had wide support among the Languedoc population and when this support tended to spread to all of France the Pope, Innocence III, sent a monk, Bernhard of Clairveaux, to preach against the heretics. He saw, however, that their services and morals were far more Christian than those of his own corrupt Church. He also admitted that he could find no fault with the *parfaits* of the Cathars. They only practised what they preached. This was not to the liking of the Pope and thus he implemented the crusade resulting in the massacre at Montségur.

Legend has it that the Holy Grail had been in the possession of the Cathars and that maybe they succeeded in getting it to safety before they surrendered to the executioners of the Inquisition. But legend did not say what the Holy Grail actually was. The general opinion was that the Grail was the cup that Yeshua had used during the Last Supper and in which, later, Joseph of Arimathea is supposed to have collected Yeshua's blood, as he was hanging on the Cross. Legend went on to say, that at one time the Grail had been in Spain, where a Moor and sufi master, Kyot of Toledo, had written about it. The first real tale of the Grail was written by Chrétien de Troyes in the 12th century, while the most well known was written by Wolfram von Eschenbach in the epic poem *Parzival*, in which the legend of King Arthur and the Knights of the Round Table was mentioned.

A common legend which had been retold for generations by the descendants of the Cathars, was told by a shepherd from Montségur as late as 1929: 'When the walls of Montségur were still intact, the Cathars, the pure ones, guarded the Holy Grail there. Montségur was in danger. The armies of Lucifer lay in a circle around the walls. They wanted the Grail, so that they could mount it in the emperor's tiara, from where it had fallen to the ground when the angels were banned from

Heaven. When peril was at its highest a white dove descended from Heaven and split the mountain in two with its beak. Esclarmonde, the female guardian of the Grail, threw the precious, holy treasure into the mountain. It then closed again. In this way the Grail was saved. When the devils forced their way into the fortress, they were too late. Filled with anger they burned all the pure ones at the foot of the cliffs under the fortress on the *camp des crémats*, on the field where the stake was built.'

Cathars, numbering 205 men, women and children, chose by their own free will to be burned at the stake. According to an oral tradition, they had promised to return after 700 years.

Early in the morning on the 29th of September I got on the train in Aarhus bound for the south of France. At half past four the next morning I got off at the small railway station in Foix. The moment I stepped down from the train and into the dense fog I realized that my reality would be changed forever. I stood still in order to find my bearings in the silence. I thought that I saw a human shape moving on the fringes of the cold, unreal light from a single lamp, only to disappear into the shadows at the end of the platform. However, I wasn't certain. All in all I wasn't certain about anything. The waiting room was empty and I couldn't see anyone as I stepped out into the sleeping town. The white, ghostly fog seemed to be the only thing alive and through a hole in it I saw what looked like a bridge. I walked that way, thinking that it may lead to the centre of the town. The sound of turbulent water assured me that I moved in the right direction. I had not gone far, however, when I was blinded by a white light, which was suddenly switched on in front of me. Then the sound of a car door being opened. I stepped out of the light and caught a faint glimpse of a person behind the wheel of a car. The person signalled to me to come closer.

'Do you need a lift?' a voice asked in beautiful English from inside the car. It was a woman. I leaned forward and muttered a 'Yes, thank you.'

'There aren't any buses at this hour,' she said. Hesitantly I got in, placed my suitcase on my lap and closed the door. In the faint light from the dashboard I saw what seemed like a smile. She then put the car into gear and swung out into the night. The headlights danced in the fog and it was like being in a spaceship on its way into an unknown universe. Neither of us spoke and I could feel that there was no need for more words. It wasn't expected. And for the first time in a very long time I felt totally relaxed and strangely free. I do not remember how far we drove. I could have continued like this forever. It was as if time disappeared and dissolved in the fog. I did notice, however, that we drove upwards and around one hairpin bend after another, as if the car found its way all by itself. Suddenly the veil was pulled away. It was an overwhelming sight as we drove out of the fog. In the light from the full moon I could now see how far up we were. Below us the mountain peaks went up through the clouds and in front of us loomed the shadow of an impressive mountain. It looked like a gigantic runic stone.

'Montségur,' she said.

I could actually sense the pride in her voice.

'This is where you get off.'

She pointed to a side road winding through some rocks.

'Just follow that.'

I was a bit confused and just managed to say thank you and goodbye as she set the car in motion. It wasn't until I was standing in the ghost-like lunar landscape, watching the car disappearing around a corner further ahead, that I realized she had not asked where I was going. How did she know that I was going to Montségur?

And what was I really doing here, since actually I could have stayed in my warm bed back home on the island? Wouldn't any normal person consider this an insane project?

The air was just as pure and cold as the moonlight. I shivered and started walking. Normal or insane – did it matter? Would it be possible to find anyone who could define the one in relation to the other? The road wound its way between the rocks. Up and up and up. At times I literally walked on the edge of the abyss. Far below, the milk-white carpet was spread across the valley. Ahead was Montségur. Off and on I could see the fortress on top of the mountain in the moonlight. It seemed as if the road was situated on a ridge circling the mountain. Something moved in the shrubs. The sound of animals disturbed by my steps, which echoed in the ice-cold air. I must have walked for about an hour when the road turned and straightened out away from the cliffs at the foot of the mountain. Below me the village of Montségur was bathed in a surreal light looking like the set in an adventure movie. From where I was I could see that, apparently, there was only the one road leading to the town. It would seem this was not a town you just travelled through. You either had business there or there was no need to make the effort of taking the road all the way around the mountain. I started the descent. The road fell in tight hairpin bends. After three quarters of an hour I finally got clear of the mountain and walked the rest of the way on the straight stretch.

The house was situated at the first corner as you came into town and you could not miss it due to the sign over the shop: Librairie 'Le Gaulois'. From the road it looked as if it was a one-storey house only. It seemed totally closed. A road continued downwards away from the town alongside the mountain and a long row of houses, which each leaned on the other. Another road turned down by another mountain also with houses built together on sloping terraces. I turned a corner and saw that the house had two-and-a-half storeys.

A few steps down was a half-open gate. A leaning figure 1, followed by a 9 in cracked enamel was fastened to the wall under a lamp with no light in it. The gate opened into a garden behind the house. I followed the steps. From the back the house looked more inviting. A window and a folding door with windowpanes, where the shutters were open. The door was locked. I then noticed another door to the right of the folding door. I knocked and turned the handle.

The door opened with a prolonged squeaking. Once inside I stood still in order to get used to the darkness. There was a faint smell of eucalyptus and roses. A raincoat was hanging on a peg. In a corner a cane and hiking boots. A flight of stairs at the end of the hall. Above it a clock and I could see that it was just past seven. I cleared my throat. I then tried with a somewhat louder hello and stood waiting in the darkness. Through an open door I could see a moonbeam shining through the window of the next room. The only sound was an electric drone from a refrigerator. I found a switch by the doorframe. It was a genuine French country kitchen with a large table in the middle of the room. Next to the kitchen sink a plate and a glass, and knives and forks in a dish drainer. Otherwise no sign of life. I went back into the hall and found another door leading into a room which most of all looked like a small banqueting hall. The outside light shone through the windows of the folding door. An enormous fireplace was the natural focal point. Two swords hung crosswise on the wall. In the middle of the room a refectory table with a bench on each side. Over the door a Cathar cross with a white dove. I went back into the hall and up the staircase. From the landing I saw a light under one of the four doors, two on each side of a long corridor. I knocked. Waited. No reaction. I opened the door. The window was ajar and here also the moon stretched its pale arms into the room, lighting it up. The room was empty except for a single mattress. There was a note on the eiderdown. 'Prat des crémats, 12 noon.' I was tired enough to sleep in a bush of thorns and my considerations whether or not to undress before going to bed were quickly done with. The last thing I remember was the mattress hitting me in the face. Then all went black.

It was a great relief when the train arrived at Gare du Nord. I had had enough of Magritte-men and digital waltzes. I had almost eight hours to find Gare du Austerlitz, where I was supposed to catch the night train for Madrid. Although the air was cool you could sense the first smell of a Parisian springtime. Outside Gare du Nord the sun stood pale and low over Boulevard de Denain, where I usually visited Brasserie 'La Consigne'. If you have only a few hours in Paris, Brasserie 'La Consigne' is the perfect place to spend them. It is as if all variations of Parisians meet here, from the retired pimp with his boxer's conk and the bleached blonde deep in conversation across two large Pernod at a table to the rear, to the young teenage girls with too much eyeliner, pigtails, peeping bellybuttons, coffee, fags, a pout and eloquent looks in the glassed-in lounge facing the boulevard. In the middle of the room the smooth dinnertime bustle with office staff, tradesmen and a single tourist, who are busy eating their lunch meal of mussels or fish soup, chocolate cake or home-made *creme de fromage*, before the next group arrives.

I found a small table in the midst of the bustle and ordered sardines with ginger and a glass of pastis. In the background Jaques Brel was singing: *Je ne sais pas pourquoi la plui, quitte lá-haut ses oripeaux ... I do not know why the rain is leaving its point, the heavy, grey clouds in the sky, in order to lay down and rest in our vineyards. I do not know why the wind is having fun spreading the laughter of the children — the frail glockenspiel of winter — in the clear mornings. I know nothing about all this; but I do know that I still love you ...*

And my thoughts danced in and out between Brel's lines. Like a very old memory, which could only be set free now. Because I knew this rain with its point and the heavy clouds in the sky, because this sky was inside of me. *Je ne sais pas pourquoi la route, qui me pousse vers la cité ... I do not know why this road is pushing me towards the town from one poplar to the next, into the warm air of the confused, or the icy cold veil of fog, which is accompanying me — why it makes me think of the cathedrals where we pray for the dead loves. I know nothing about all this; but I do know that I still love you ...* Because I knew that I had sat in this brasserie and looked at all these faces so many times before. If not there, then somewhere like it. I knew that I had been there and listened to their voices talking about defeats and lies, hectic screws, infidelity and jealousy so often, that perhaps my own heart had grown distant and hard. And I had thought that I had put all this behind me. Perhaps I was finally looking towards another kind of future, unused and new. And then it happened. *Je ne sais pas pourquoi la ville ... I do not know why the town is opening up its suburban ramparts in order to let me slide quietly under the rain between its lovers — in all my frailty. I do not know why all these people have their noses glued to the windowpanes in order better to celebrate my defeat — in order better to follow my funeral procession. I know nothing about all this; but I do know that I still love you.*

Maybe now I finally understood that all these destinies were not merely stories taking place in a fictitious world outside of me. They were all me. The masks and the characters. The streets and the towns. The beggars and the train stations. The songs and the wind. The longing. *Je ne sais pas pourqoui ces rues ... I do not know why these streets are opening up in front of me one by one, virginal and cold, cold and naked. Nothing is there but my own steps and there is no moon. I do not know why the night has forced me to come here in order to cry in front of this train station, by strumming me like a guitar. I know nothing about all this; but I do know that I still love you.*

This was everything I thought I had forgotten – the memory of longing – which had finally caught up with me. And at the end of the galled and hardened voice of Jacques Brel, right at the edge of this world's amusement park, the terminal station of everything, I let go of all the artificial finery, since I was just travelling through and perhaps I did not need to remember anything else. *Je ne sais rien de tout cela, mais je sais que je t'aime encore.*

The House

4

I woke from my dream because the rain was beating against the windowpane. The water trickled in the gutter and sang in the down-pipes outside. A grey light moved lazily across the cracked ceiling. In the corner a small porcelain clown sat smiling in his cream-coloured eternity. In my dream I had been giving a concert for my fellow patients at the asylum for the mentally ill, where I was admitted. I had built the piano I was playing on from conches and I had tuned it with a ladle. When I played, the notes turned into drops of water and the music into rain, which could make you psychic if it got into your eyes. Just before the finale the concert was interrupted because the professor had just found out that the piece I was playing wasn't written by anyone. Then I woke up.

I stayed in bed hoping to hear the sound of people; but I only heard the rain. Then I got up and went downstairs.

It was just before 11. There was a toilet and a shower in a corridor behind the banqueting hall. I took a badly needed shower. Afterwards I found a kettle in the kitchen and boiled some water. Someone had placed freshly baked bread on the table. Under it a map of the area. A red line marked the road to 'Prat de crémats'. I found a piece of goat's cheese in the refrigerator. I cut a few slices of bread, made tea and noticed that the dish drainer was empty. In the hall both the raincoat and the boots were still there. I was not surprised to find that they fitted me perfectly. I pulled the hood over my head as I walked out into the pouring rain.

The town seemed ghostlike. Many houses were closed for the winter, but smoke came out of several chimneys and fused into the grey clouds. A wet cat was licking itself in an open shed. The beat from a hammer echoed from the cliff wall in the cold air. Craftsmen were putting a new roof on a house situated on the slope of the mountain. An old Citröen stood on a ledge leaking oil, which mixed with the rain and made purple stripes on the tarmac. A dog barked in the vicinity. I passed the cemetery and started walking along the same winding road by which I had arrived.

It took about 20 minutes. I began feeling the rigours of the night. Every step hurt. When I reached the parking place at the foot of the mountain, a granite stairway led up to some bushes and a few trees. According to the map this was the only path leading to the fortress. It had stopped raining. Making my way through the bushes I suddenly felt something cold in my face. An impulse? The presence of an invisible power? A whisper? *Give me your heart!* A flicker of light between the trees. A soft vibration in front of me. A movement in the air. I stopped. Closed my eyes and took a deep breath. It felt as if I was being carried by invisible hands. I then stepped into an open space. *Prat des crémats!*

A man was standing in the middle of the meadow facing

me. He was too far away for me to see his features. But I had no doubt at all that this was the Seer. Behind him the mountain was waiting. At the top the fortress was waiting. In the fortress ... ?

It was as if all the corners of the world moved towards the figure at the centre. Like a centripetal force whirling everything around. I had stopped noticing my steps, but I felt that I floated towards him. I could now see his face. His beret. The white beard. The mysterious smile. The eyes! The eyes that sucked me into the power of the eternal centre. And in that moment I knew that there was no going back and that everything was exactly as it was supposed to be.

'Do you always make such a commotion when you arrive somewhere?' he said with a smile and stuck his cane into the ground in front of him.

'One might think that you were expected.'

He waved his arms about:

'Welcome to Prats place. It was here that 205 men, women and children voluntarily went to the stake. If you can imagine that?'

He pointed to the fortress.

'What is up there is important. But not until you understand what happened down here.'

He pointed to the ground in front of him. I was watching him. It was impossible to see how old he was. He might be 60 or 100. But his movements were agile like those of a young man. There was an aura of calm about him. As if he himself was a mountain. All my tensions and reservations were gone like morning dew. There was an openness in his voice which made me feel safe. A solicitude that went right through you and into your core. It was as if it restored everything that had been upset in you and removed everything that shouldn't be there.

'Why am I here?' I heard myself asking. The question hovered in the air like a bird shot in its flight. He smiled.

He knew that I knew the answer even before I had put the question to him.

'It was just a matter of time before we met,' he said. 'The time has come, and this is where it should happen.'

He looked at me and my eyes melted into his. It seemed totally unreal. It was like looking into an endless universe where time was no more. The black eyes were illuminated galaxies that had been travelling since time immemorial to manifest here in a meadow in southern France. All this lasted for just a moment. But a moment which had been forever. Like throwing a glance and this glance sees everything. I could see a shape mirrored in his eyes, and I realized that it was me. Flames reached towards the sky from an enormous bonfire behind me.

'What happened?' I asked.

'A decision was made. It is the traditional understanding of what death is that blurs our understanding. We see nothing but the fear in the faces of those pushed towards the flames, we hear nothing but the screams of the condemned. But this is not what is essential. The Cathars made a choice. They might have returned to their villages and continued to live their lives as usual, if they'd been willing to renounce what they knew to be true and then convert to the Church of Rome. But they refused to do that. They chose the stake. Apparently, they had a knowledge that went further than the traditional meaning of what life and death meant.'

His words were muffled and came directly at me. They made me remember. I myself had once been tied to the stake surrounded by flames. That is why I knew that the stake was just an external manifestation of the limitations connected with mortal life. That the pain and the transition from one situation to another last for a short moment only. That there was another meaning to it.

The Mountain

'Now it's your turn to make a decision. That is why you have come. You have been studying for 20 years. You have been thinking and writing. You know all the mystics, all the various traditions. You've experienced flashes of the other reality. But until now, it has all been like a lifelong flirtation. You didn't know how to make any use of it. It's high time that you made your choice. There is still time to go back to the comfort of your spiritual and religious fascination. You'll probably learn to be happy as time goes by. But then again, you may as well start collecting stamps.'

A bird screeched close by.

'You can also choose to take the path.'

He pointed to the path disappearing between the bushes and continuing its way up the mountain.

'If you choose that, you choose the stake.'

He hesitated and continued more quietly:

'I shall start you on your path and show you your possibilities. Hand you your freedom. But before you make your choice you must know, that if you follow me now you must be ready to learn everything over again. Do not believe that walking the path is the same as living a carefree life. Quite the opposite.'

For the first time he looked away. It was as if a chasm opened between us. It was my choice and mine alone. He turned around and started walking. I looked at him while thoughts were spinning in my head. He stopped 50 metres away. I could almost feel the flames. I was thinking that if I was to tell anyone about this it would seem totally absurd. Sparks flew in the air. They were everywhere. They looked like angels and they danced above the Seer's head. The whole place was filled with them. Suddenly I was in doubt. In all the accounts I had read about mystics, they warned about these kinds of experiences. They thought that they were the work of the devil – illusions created to lead people to believe that they had seen something divine; that at worst it might make them arrogant and make them feel above others.

It looked like a firework display. And in the middle of everything stood the Seer smiling his unfathomable smile. Illusions or not, I took a step forward.

'This is where you may meet Prat, the female guardian of nature.' he said when I got close to him.

'She is standing in front of you and is saying that she's been waiting for you a long time. Your time has come, and you must acknowledge that you must accept your task and that you must complete it. She says that she is your guardian.'

He stepped aside. I was looking into space. I tried to squint but didn't succeed. She wasn't there. I closed my eyes. I made the greatest effort. Where were the angels now? It was completely quiet. Most of all, I wanted to open my eyes and disappear into the wonderful fireworks around me, but I forced myself to keep standing there looking into the darkness. I don't know for how long I stayed like this. My thoughts went in all directions. It felt like coasting down a very long and steep hill on a bicycle without knowing if the brakes were working. Then I also let go of the bicycle that disappeared under me and left me floating in a different form of wakefulness. I thought I spotted the outline of a girl in front of me but it was vague and it disappeared before I could maintain it. The moment the picture disappeared I felt something cool, similar to my experience when I walked through the bushes. I opened my eyes and looked around. The Seer had gone and so had the fireworks. I spotted a figure well on its way up the mountain. It was him. He was waiting in the same agile, alert and relaxed way, his cane in front of him but now about half a kilometre away. This was impossible! I started walking. The beginning of the path went in a straight line. Bare and steep with a sandy and loose surface which made it even more difficult to walk on. I was completely exhausted when I reached him.

'How did you get up here so fast?' I asked him, out of breath. But, the question that really burned in me was more what was I doing here. He stood for a while looking at Prat des crémats below us. Then he looked at me. He totally ignored my question and instead answered what was on my mind.

'You are here to set foot where most people dare not go. It is your task to travel into the unknown, to penetrate into the mystery about eternity in man, to reveal new possibilities and to write home about it. You are a kind of explorer, if you like.'

He saw right through me. Perhaps I ought to have felt frightened, but I didn't. It seemed quite natural.

'But you still have to make up your mind about a few things and to put them behind you, before you can travel freely.'

He stepped in among the bushes and pulled out a backpack and gave it to me.

'Put it on.'

I looked at him questioningly. What was going on?

'Just do what I say,' he said with an encouraging smile.

Slightly bewildered I took it and began strapping it onto my back. He bent down and picked up a stone. It was the size of a fist.

'This stone symbolizes your reluctance to accept your right place in life.'

He put the stone into the backpack and bent down to pick up another, which he showed me.

'This represents your reservations in regard to other people.'

He bent down once more.

'This, your unclarified relationship to your parents.'

And yet another one.

'This, your unclarified relationship to women.'

He then searched carefully until he found one that seemed

right. He showed it to me and it was quite a bit bigger than the others:

'This one symbolizes all your unimportant and unnecessary worries.'

It was added to the others and I could feel the straps cutting into my shoulders. He bent down again and came up with a stone that was even bigger than the previous one:

'This one is for all the mistakes you have ever made and all the shortcomings you feel are still a part of you.'

I had to lean forward to compensate for the backward pull and was about to protest as he handed me another couple of stones:

'There are only three more to go. They all represent the guilt and the fear of life expressed in you as cowardice – arrogance – and self-righteousness.'

One by one he placed them on top of the others pondering each word carefully. I could feel the anger boiling inside of me. What did he know about all this? It was exactly this that I felt I had been working so intensely with. I really wanted to stop this circus and walk away. Instead I set my teeth, leaned forward stubbornly in order to get a better grip on the straps of my backpack, which by now was very heavy. Deep down I knew that he was right.

'Now, focus your thoughts on the burden you carry on your shoulders. Think about each and every stone and what it symbolizes. Each one is a part of what holds you in chains and restricts your freedom. They represent all that keeps you from moving freely about, to do what you came to do.

'Before coming to Monségur you worked with these things on an intellectual level, but were unable to let them go. That is the reason for your illness. You have to relate to your problems in a truer way. You are now going to carry them for the last time. Together we will climb this mountain to find the spot where you will let all of it go.'

He turned around and started climbing. I followed him.

The path narrowed. Further up it began winding its way between rocks, scrubs and bushes. The stones we walked on were slippery from the rain and I had to concentrate on each step. In front of me the Seer almost floated upwards while my own boots became more and more heavy. Off and on, the path almost disappeared because of the rain, and I had to press against the face of the cliff and hold my balance from ledge to ledge. At other places it widened again and became fairly safe and stable to walk on. My burden became more and more real. By now, I was bending over so far, that I almost crawled upwards. I was sweating profusely. As promised by the Seer, I now felt the physical weight of all that had been the psychological burden of my life. Carrying them up the mountain, all the shortcomings, reservations and projections were made real in a way that forced me to look at them. It was impossible to repress them now, because they quite literally cut into my shoulders, bent my back and made my legs wobble beneath me. And crawling forward I began to understand the meaning of this apparently pointless task. I suddenly felt responsible for all these ailments. It all of a sudden became important to me that they were brought safely to wherever they were supposed to go. I was totally soaked with sweat and reeling when finally we made a halt on a wide ledge.

'No more today,' the Seer said.

I was about to take off my backpack; but he stopped me.

'Wait – come over here and enjoy the view.'

I went over to the edge. The cliff wall went straight down. The valley spread out below us looking like a fairy tale. On the other side the Spanish part of the snow-topped Pyrenees showed itself. An eagle soared across the sky. The Cathar landscape spread beautifully on both sides as far as we could see. I could see the fortress high above us. It was still far away.

He reached across my shoulder and into the backpack and took out a stone, which he handed to me:

'Now, take your self-righteousness. Hold it in your hand. Feel it. What do you want with it? It is totally unimportant. Forget it! Drop it!'

He pointed to the edge. I closed my eyes, holding it and feeling its smooth surface. Feeling its weight. I could suddenly understand what had nurtured it and why I had felt it necessary to hide behind it.

'Your self-righteousness has now served its purpose. Although it will reappear in a new disguise you'll be able to recognize it and know what to do with it. Today you have decided to let it go forever. You have made a choice.'

I opened my hand and let the stone fall from it. It hit a protruding piece of cliff and fell into the deep chasm.

'And here is your arrogance.'

He handed it to me. This one was also smooth and cold. It was round as a ball and I put it up to my cheekbone like a shot-putter. I blessed it and sent it out into nothingness forever.

'Your cowardice.'

He handed me a big and dry one with edges, which felt blunt and unwieldy. A shapeless monument of infamy to my equally shapeless feelings of guilt and fear which had caused so much chaos.

'You have dissolved it by finding the courage to carry it up here in the first place. You can let it go now.'

I let it fall.

'Here are all your shortcomings.'

It was a big and warm stone, which was both angular and round. It felt right in my hand and it had a nice feel to it.

'Those are the shortcomings that are the reason you are here today. Without them you would have experienced nothing and learned nothing. There's a lot to be grateful for. But now you have outgrown them and you must let them go.'

The Seer

I stood for a long time with the stone in my hand. In a way it represented what until now had been a stabilizing factor in my life. But it had also been a pleasant possibility of escape. I kissed it and threw it over the edge. It drew a fine curve in the air and disappeared.

'Your unimportant and unnecessary worries.'

The stone was cold with sharp edges. This one also represented escape and fear. I made a run-up and threw it with all my force.

'Your crippled way of relating to women.' he said with a smile.

I now saw that this stone looked phallic more or less. This apparently, was a kind of graphic education, where the point quite literally was carved in stone. I held it at arm's length. It was funny.

Screamingly funny. I couldn't help laughing, and we both laughed with tears running down our cheeks.

'A so-called stand-up comedian!' he said when I kissed the petrified phallus and, still laughing, threw it into the abyss.

I knew, of course, that it was more serious than that. But our laughter somehow gave it all the proper perspective. It became clear that my way of relating to women had something to do with a path or a power in me, that I had not yet acknowledged. Once more it seemed as if the Seer could read my mind.

'Tomorrow you may meet Prat. Then you will know,' he said and reached for yet another stone:

'This stone represents your unclarified relationship with your parents.'

I took it, and although it was scarred after many beatings, it was also warm and a perfect work of art.

'You must now forgive them all the shortcomings that you've quite consciously blamed them for, and hope that they'll also forgive you your silent accusations and rejections.'

The words went straight to my heart. Suddenly I could see it all quite clearly. My parents and the circumstances they acted from. Their relentless battle to build a life matching all the expectations and all the standards they felt they had to live up to. All their losses and disappointments. And in the middle of it all, their care and stubborn will to get there, in spite of it all. I let go and watched the stone slide down the mountainside until it was out of sight.

'Finally, these two. Your relationship to other people and the way you relate to your present task.'

I took the stones one in each hand, and weighed them against each other. They were about equally heavy. It would be a waste of time to hold on to them. I let go of them at the same time and heard the echo as they struck the cliff wall further down.

'Well, that's it,' I said and looked across the valley.

It was completely quiet. Only the whisper of the wind was heard between the cliffs like the sound from a conch that you hold against your ear. The sound of heaven and of freedom. The impossible had happened. Not only did I feel liberated and relieved, but for the first time ever I felt no guilt for having these feelings. It was not a practical joke. This was serious. It worked. It was through the manifesting of all my problems as physical burdens, which I could change or discard, that the sense of liberation and relief was able to reach my inner self. No matter how I looked at it, no matter how many excuses came to mind, it was impossible to deny that on a completely tangible level I had now made peace with deeply distressing elements from my past. In spite of severe pains in my joints and muscles I was filled with a well-being that I had never known before. I turned around to offer my thanks, only to find that he was gone. I listened. But heard only the wind and the silence. I thought I could see a tiny shape at the outskirts of Prat des crémats far below, but was unsure. Under normal circumstances I would have sworn it was impossible he could have gone that far. But now, I didn't know what to believe.

The descent from the mountain was as long and as difficult as the ascent had been, and when finally I got back to the village it was getting dark. I was totally exhausted. Someone had turned the light on in the kitchen. I practically fell into a chair and had to sit for quite a long time before I felt myself again. I barely managed to have some bread and goat's cheese. I do not remember how I got into bed.

5

The tube under Gare du Nord was like a silent, unrelenting sea. Endless rivers of individuals kept appearing, tumbling up and down stairs, flowing between ticket counters and turnstiles and splitting into smaller rivers heading for various destinations: Bobigny, Pablo Picasso, Place d'Italie, Porte de Clignancourt, Porte d'Orleans, Orly or Aéroport de Gaulle. I remembered everything from my trip to Montségur half a year earlier and followed the river and the signs to the platform for Place d'Italie. Everywhere masks of despair, downcast and expressionless eyes, brief, silent and haunted looks. Legions of boots and shoes hammering through ice-cold passages, sometimes to the right, sometimes to the left and others straight ahead. The last, long passage towards the platform was black with people. Black with people dead behind the eyes. I was the only living person in sight. Had it been six months earlier then I would have kept step, since I myself was black in my soul. I now stepped out of the river, pressed against the wall and stayed there. Maybe to break or underline the apparent symbolism.

Se tiennent par la main et marchent en silence ... They are holding hands and are walking in silence in these extinct cities brought into an equilibrium by the drizzle of the rain. Nothing can be heard except their singing steps, step by step. They walk silently, the broken-hearted. Who else but Jacques Brel could have written this song for the film *Les Désespérés*?

Ils ont brûlé leurs ailes ils ont perdu leurs branches ... They have scorched their wings, they have lost their branches, shipwrecked to a degree that death seems white. They return out of love, they have been awakened, they march in despair, the broken-hearted. I wonder if Brel was conscious about this picture when he created it? Did he know that death here in the tube at Place d'Italie, quite literally, was white, because he himself once stood here pressed against the wall?

Et je sais leur chemin pour l'avoir cheminé ... And I know their road because I have walked it myself, by now more than a hundred times, a hundred times more than halfway, less aged or more bruised they would have ended it. They walk in silence, the broken-hearted.

The train was packed. People standing and sitting – almost on top of each other. I was sucked in when they whistled for departure and the doors slid to. Turned-away faces. Downcast eyes. Eyes shut. The smell of clothes and coins. Skin and anger. Poverty and sex. Violence and longing. The rocking of the train. Gare l'Est, Jacques Bonsergent, République. Like a river that kept overflowing. At Oberkampf a mass of tributaries, the last downfall of the lonely, the iron fist of disappointment, the losing dance, a falling shadow in the long chorus of oblivion. Richard Lenoir, Bréguet Sabin. Bastille. Stanza after stanza – man's endless and short-sighted song to destiny. Or was it destiny's short but endlessly repeated song to us? A stranger in transit got off at Gare d'Austerlitz and went up to get a cup of coffee and a glass of pastis at Saint-Germain-des Prés. *Ils marchent en silence les désespérés.*

It rained all morning. I woke up while it was still dark. Down in the kitchen I lit a candle and sat watching the day being born. Perhaps I finally understood that *being* was only possible when you can accept that it doesn't entail being anything in particular. That this really is the most beautiful way of being anything at all. That the abandonment of the eternal chase for recognition and confirmation is a decisive condition for the gaining of peace. To be able to be out of sight and therefore to be unnoticed by others. To be able to sit quietly in an unknown darkness far away from the attention of other people. To be able to focus on yourself without being egocentric, and then expand your consciousness to a degree that it may contain something other than your own self, which is convinced it is the master of the world. A condition where the ideas of subjectivity and objectivity begin to dissolve.

Everything that the Seer had helped me to let go of on the mountain had opened up to something else. As he told me, anyone can get up and publicly air lofty ethics and a fine sounding morality. Saying one thing and doing something else is a part of the lie and psychological make-up accepted by humanity. But what thoughts and what ethics move the same person in solitude and without an audience? Is it at all possible to stay alive without being seen and being heard?

What I had let go on the mountain had opened up to a condition, where it became possible to be satisfied with just sitting unnoticed in the dusk, listening to the blessed monotony of the rain. Without any other need than just remaining there. Perhaps this condition was part of what the Seer had told me to study and write about. Simply because otherwise people would not know it existed. Perhaps it didn't seem like much. It was probably nothing. Not very fascinating. It could not be bought or sold. But, precisely because of that, it might be important – that you might to find peace by doing nothing. Not necessarily as a permanent condition, but a kind of state from where you might reach something important. Maybe it was the house? Maybe it was the village or the mountain? Maybe it existed in another time or outside of time? Somehow, I had always lived there and always known that it existed, because it had always been there as a possibility in me. It was the same with the Seer. Although I had spent one day only with him, it felt as if I had always known him. The fact that I had met him just now was simply an expression of the perfect timing of an age-old yet timeless Andalusian manuscript.

After a shower, as I was drying myself, I thought I heard sounds from the kitchen followed by the front door being closed. I quickly tied the towel around me and ran to the glass door in the great hall. I was just in time to see a woman disappearing through the garden gate. Returning to the kitchen I found a parcel on the table containing freshly baked bread and some goat's cheese. Apparently there was no end to the fairy tale.

Outside the wind started to blow. I made breakfast and began writing in my diary. The shutters moaned on their hinges. I had written a couple of pages when I felt this strange cold wind touching my face. I looked up but no one was there. At this moment one of the shutters hit the window with a bang and left the kitchen in darkness. I stayed in my chair listening intensely, but the only sound was the wind playing with the open shutters in my room upstairs. I nevertheless felt that someone was in the room. I groped for the matches on the table, but overturned my cup splashing tea over everything. The chair fell over backwards when I got up to reach for the matches, which I knew were on the kitchen range. I lit a candle and was just in time to save my diary before it became soaked in tea. I was startled when I saw him. He sat at the end of the table almost outside the circle of light, smiling his subtle smile.

'How did you get in?' I asked open-mouthed.

I must have looked ridiculous as it was very difficult for him to keep his laughter back. I took a dishcloth and wiped the table.

'Let us say that I wanted to test your elegance,' he said and continued, 'I wanted a cup of coffee and thought that because of the weather you might want a lift to the mountain.'

He got up and poured boiling water into a cup with instant coffee. Outside, we could hear the fury of the elements. I was thinking that if this house, this town, well, the whole area didn't exist in another reality, then it might not exist at all.

'Don't worry. This is more real than you can imagine.'

Once more he had read my thoughts, and once again he did not answer the question I had put to him.

'But how's it possible that you suddenly appear in this kitchen without any sound and without being seen?'

This time I wasn't going to let him off the hook. He hesitated and then said 'It is all a matter of balance. But you'll soon know.'

He opened the window and pushed the shutters open. The grey light filled the kitchen.

'You have already started on this part of it. You're contemplating to what degree you'll be able to just *be* and do nothing. A part of you finds it is appropriate, while another part is protesting loudly. There is a little man inside you who feels you can't live unless you fill your life with a cornucopia of intense and nervous activity. Since this activity must have another purpose than just fulfilling the needs of this little man, he invents a series of positive purposes to work towards.

But they constitute nothing except his alibi for continuing his escape and maintaining a high degree of consumption. Of course he also finds it's important to help the poor of the Third World and abolish wars and all that. That's one of the reasons he's so busy. He's not considering the fact that it is precisely his own over-consumption that's indirectly causing most of the wars. And also that it's impounding most of the resources which otherwise could have benefited the Third World.'

He rinsed his cup and placed it in the dish tray. I felt that I had to protest and had a strange urge to play the devil's advocate:

'You can't just sit down and just *be*, and then leave everything alone.'

'You can't?'

He turned towards me and looked into my eyes.

'But who's going to keep the wheels turning, and where is everything going to come from?' I asked.

'You wait and see.'

We drove in his car. A dark-green Chrysler Vision. I couldn't help thinking that this also represented some kind of extravagance and was about to comment on it. But he got in first.

'Well, I'm sorry,' he said, 'I'm probably a romantic, but a realistic kind of romantic. You only see the items. You see the brand of the car. Today this car is ours. Tomorrow somebody else may drive it. It has been a part of my home for a couple of months now. It is useful when you work at great altitudes.'

He smiled and continued:

'It's all a matter of balance. At any given moment to be able to let go. Not to let yourself become attached to anything. To be able to distinguish. To be flexible.'

It took only ten minutes. He parked the car between some

bushes. The wind had died down, but the sky was black and it looked as if it might open its floodgates at any moment.

'You'd better take this,' he said and handed me a black cane with an interlacing pattern.

'Today we take it one step further up.'

He didn't waste any time.

'Today I want to show you Prat, and we can only hope that she also wants to see you. I'll go through the thicket first and you follow immediately. When you feel a slight electric-like shiver down your spine, you'll know that she's present.

'But you won't be able to see her. Instead, you must tell yourself that you want to be isogynic. Do you understand? It is important that you do understand this. The isogynic condition is, in a way, a neutral condition. Don't be afraid if you feel you are beginning to dissolve. When you get through the bramble, stand still and concentrate on being isogynic. It is a mind leap. It is an icon. In the isogynic state you are free from being either man or woman, you are not one or the other, you are both and none of them. It has got nothing to do with the androgynous or sexuality. It is a beautiful condition. Open, free, transcendent and flexible. It's not enough to imagine the condition, you must become it. I'll let you know when you can move on from there. Do you understand?'

He looked directly into me. The light played in his black eyes. I nodded. He turned around and walked towards the bramble. Suddenly he seemed very serious, which I had not noticed before. I followed him until he was out of sight.

The bramble closed around me. The branches seemed alive. I walked with my eyes closed and concentrated as much as possible. But my thoughts were all a shambles and went this way and that. I kept repeating: I am isogynic, I am isogynic. A gust of wind went through the thicket. I stopped, had doubts. Was this her? A movement? A whisper? *Give me your heart!* It felt like a slight touch. I recognized this feather-light touch. In a series of very quick movements layer after layer was removed inside me. I tried instinctively to fight it, but I couldn't. It happened as fast as the last drop of water sucked from the plughole of a bathtub. You notice it, but you are not sufficiently fast with the plug, before the water is gone. In a flash I realized that I was neither the bathtub nor the water running out. I was the *emptiness* in the bathtub, the empty space, the openness that the water had filled just a moment ago.

He was standing in the middle of the open space. Exactly as the day before. I stayed at the outskirts and waited for a sign. The wind had died down. There was a hypnotic silence everywhere. Then the lines started drawing towards him. Slowly at first, in a gliding movement, but then faster and faster without any sound. Once more I felt the sense of floating as I moved closer to him.

'Very well,' he said as I stood in front of him looking into an endless universe.

His seriousness apart, I felt that he was now also very determined.

'Please listen very carefully, I have no intention of repeating this. There is so much to show you here. Prat tells me that you are well known to her. You are a lonely wanderer. You have been misunderstood and mistreated. You don't want that anymore. You are standing here, beaten and perplexed. But if this was not so, you would not have come. There is a connection between everything. You have just now, without any seeming difficulty, moved in and out of the isogynic condition. Your time has come. It is totally up to you if you want to go all the way. Prat tells me that you have the opportunity now, but you must seize it now if you are serious. You may not get another.'

The galaxies shone. I could feel his eyes all the way into empty space. Then he stepped aside. I stood still with my eyes closed but felt right away that this wasn't right. When I opened them again she stood directly in front of me. Prat. The quintessence of compassion. This universal being represented the essence of womanhood in all its various shapes and ages. I saw her as the girl on a throne. The feminine force. The guardian of the Grail, Esclarmonde? She got up, walked towards me and embraced me. She took my heart and filled it with tenderness. A kind of tenderness that I did not know existed. Here is your heart! I saw a sparrow sitting on the ground in front of me. It hopped back and forth for a while. Then it flew away. She was gone.

It took but a few moments. Still, I wasn't surprised to see that the Seer, like the day before, had already passed the initial, steep part of the climb. He waved at me. I started thinking how helpful it would be if I also could learn to fly.

We began the ascent. Although I no longer had a backpack heavy with stones, it was still an exhausting climb. The Seer walked upright and effortless in front of me, and I concentrated on the heels of his boots, just to keep up. Getting up part of the way, I could see black clouds hovering towards us. Lightning flashed now and then and you could hear the thunder getting louder and louder. We were about halfway up when the rain fell and, apparently, there was nowhere to seek shelter. The Seer signalled to me that we should carry on, but further ahead he stepped away from the path and found his way under a ledge hidden behind a few bushes.

'We can find shelter here,' he said shaking the water off.

We sat down on two pieces of rock and admired the landscape stretched out in front of us. The rain poured down as he broke the silence:

'Are you hungry?'

Before I had time to answer he pointed behind me, where I saw two bottles of water and a metal box, filled with biscuits, between the rocks.

'They are very far-sighted – the Norns,' he said, when I handed him a bottle of water and a few biscuits.

'The Norns?'

I must have looked quite foolish considering his familiar smile.

'Didn't you notice them?' he replied, drinking from the bottle.

I looked around but couldn't see anyone. He laughed noisily and I tried again.

'Urd, Verdante, Skuld?' I asked.

He nodded. Of course I knew the Fatal Sisters from the Nordic mythology, Past, Present and Future. The Norns who spin, measure and cut the thread of life for each individual. But what were they doing here?

'Who do you think supplies breakfast for strange fugitives visiting as remote a place as Montségur?' he asked teasingly. 'Or meet strange persons like yourself at the railway station of Foix in the middle of the night? Or hide supplies between the rocks for two madmen like us on a mountain during a thunderstorm?'

He flung his arms about, but became serious again.

'Urd is saying that your past has contained a lot of fear. Your life has been marked by a deep sense of feeling abandoned and lonely. You've never been able to feel at home anywhere. Neither here nor there. Verdante says that you have now left the spiral fog in order to manifest your true qualities.'

His eyes were like needles.

'Skuld is saying that you will be ready for the task in the future, because you know how to work in solitude and how to work secretly. She also says that you must retreat if anyone pushes you too far or exceeds your personal barriers. You are here to offer new possibilities. It is, however, very important that you work freely and without any kind of limitations.'

He emptied his bottle and got up. The rain had stopped and the air was fresh and cool.

'I'm glad I don't have to tell anyone about all this,' I said and followed him.

Girl on Throne
(Thomas Gotsch, 1894)

'Who says that you don't?' He walked to the edge and looked across the valley. He then brushed his hands against each other and made a sign for us to continue. The path was even more slippery now after the rain and we progressed only slowly. I was considering what he had just said. But how was I to tell anyone about this. Most people would think that I had lost it. On the other hand, what did that matter? I would almost certainly be dismissed as it was. And why should I take this into consideration anyway, just to look good in the eyes of others? Wasn't life too short to keep silent and to hide things?

We struggled upwards and rested on a ledge further up. He turned to me:

'This is where we find the Oracle. This is where you may ask your question and receive the answer yourself. You might as well learn it now. I'll ask the same question and we'll see if I get the same answer.'

He motioned me forward.

'You must ask your question loud and clear.'

I took a step forward with my eyes closed and was just about to start, as he interrupted:

'No, you must open your eyes. This is important.'

I opened my eyes and stood still and tried to concentrate. I then noticed an eagle soaring ahead of me. It was on the lookout for prey. Then I asked:

'How do I continue from here?'

I hadn't thought much about the question. It just seemed to come into my mind. I followed the eagle with my eyes. It circled and circled, ready to strike. I sensed the intensity around it. It was totally concentrated on its task and would soon unite with its prey. Then it swooped down and at that moment I received the answer. Like lightning.

'Did you get an answer?' he asked.

'I think so,' I replied.

He nodded with a satisfied look on his face:

'Good, here is my version.'

He stood for a while looking straight ahead, then continued:

'You must travel alone and without any unnecessary luggage. At this present stage of the voyage you must not visit anyone, not even those similarly disposed. The process of dissolution that you have experienced over the last years is at an end. You must now travel freely, work in silence and develop your powers of thought. You must write about it later on.'

I was totally dumbfounded. This was exactly the answer I had received myself. Maybe not precisely in the same wording, but there was no doubt about the contents. He looked at the sky. It still looked black and menacing. He said:

'We will not walk further today. Tomorrow we'll take it yet another step higher.'

I looked up at the fortress. Then I spotted the eagle. It soared through the air, circled once and settled in a tree on a ledge next to ours. It was carrying something. A sparrow.

We had our supper at Gilbert's. Gilbert was the proprietor of the Hotel Costes, a small business, which had been in the hands of the family for generations. It was a humble place with a few rooms upstairs and a few tables in the restaurant, which was run on very simple principles: Gilbert's wife, Maurisette, in the kitchen, Gilbert himself serving the meals each day, eight months a year. Full satisfaction or your money wasted.

At one of the tables two middle-aged couples were having trout. A smell of vinegar and aniseed. An old radio was playing a scratched version of old, French dance hall music, interrupted by a voice trying to get through from a time long forgotten. We were greeted with open arms. Gilbert took the Seer's hands in both his, squeezed them and shook them over and over while words and laughter filled the room. He called

Maurisette into the restaurant so that she could also welcome us. We had hardly sat down at the table before two glasses of pastis and a carafe of water were placed in front of us. The Seer raised his glass to me:

'Such a welcome is rare even among the closest of friends.'

We drank.

Maurisette and Gilbert understand the simple and the uncompli-cated. You may have meat and vegetables or fish and vegetables or just vegetables. That's the menu. Simple all the way. All eight months. This is the essence of respect. This they show by making certain that one feels at home. They do that by the quality of the food and the very reasonable prices. All the primary produce is from the local area. It is first and foremost a way of life, the business is secondary.

We drank to each other again. Gilbert behind his table, beaming like the sun. Nobody should be in doubt that tonight he had a very important and highly treasured guest.

Gilbert served fish. The Seer had brought wine from Don Cesar in Spain. He gave Gilbert several bottles. More guests arrived. The arthritic dance music boomed like a funfair filled with bustle and noise. Maurisette appeared and turned it down. As soon as she was out of sight, Gilbert turned it up again. They laughed and drank to each other. The Seer said:

'Every perfection has its flaw. No system is infallible. Even great truths know about the little white lie! He pointed to his plate:

'Here, even the fish can fly.'

6

I walked in the drizzle along Jardin des Plantes on my way to Boulevard Saint-Germain. I was thinking whether or not I had the time to visit 14 Rue Abbé de l'Épée, where the Danish author Herman Bang used to stay, when Paris was his second home. I knew the place and had been there several times, but for some reason I decided against it. Perhaps because I suddenly and for no apparent reason had found myself in the songs of Brel. Although in many ways they resembled the writings of Bang, they belonged to another era. Or maybe I had lost that particular thread because I was presently reading the collected works of Georges Simenon. Perhaps I was descending into a far deeper memory which had not necessarily anything to do with Paris but which, for reasons unknown, could only be redeemed here. I had experienced such situations since childhood, but I never knew beforehand when they would arise. They were kind of holes in time, openings to another reality or to a parallel universe. As a child I had experienced transcendence into other eras. I had seen deceased persons come alive. I had seen past and future incidents played out in front of me, without realizing what it was until much later. I had felt other people's sorrows as my own just by looking at them. Many times had I seen the reasons for them. Through these openings I often wandered unnoticed out of time and into other worlds. I could never tell what activated the memory and what created the opening. It might be a person, a pair of eyes, a mouth, a scent or a sound. It might be an item, a letter or the way in which the rain fell. It might be a place, a street, a house, or the way the light shone. It might be a word, a song, or the way two people passed each other. I could be walking down a street when suddenly I had the choice either to continue towards the destination I had set out for or follow a sudden impulse, which might lead through a gate and into a backyard, or to getting on a bus going in the opposite direction. It has always been like this with me and books, that if I didn't find them, they found me. In a bookstore, for example, I might walk directly to a bookcase and pull out the exact book that I needed at that moment. If it didn't seem like it at the beginning, I could be quite certain that somewhere in the book there would be references to the one I needed. At other times they might quite literally fall on my head or arrive by mail. I had never considered it to be particularly unusual at all. It was just a part of the things that one didn't talk about. Little by little I learned to keep those things to myself. It was downright embarrassing when someone bent forks and made clocks stop by the simple power of thought on television. It was very strange when someone wanted to upset the two most important inventions of man, utensils for eating and time. I supposed that no one had seen the same person straightening the forks out again or making the clocks go again. All such showmanship made people with the same kinds of abilities play them down or keep silent about them.

It was not until Montségur that the Seer showed me how these time holes could be used as convenient escape routes, through which I could disappear each time reality became too insistent. They might also be linked to the periods of time when I was ill. He had shown me how these loopholes, which usually lead to the lower astral conditions, could instead be transformed into openings to a present reality; openings, so to speak, turning inward towards the now of things instead of outward and away from them. By sharpening my attention and intensifying it, every time these situations arose, I would eventually come to master them. In this way I would eventually be able to develop the inner resonance and the inner sight, which was a prerequisite to being able to move freely through other dimensions. But as things were right now, I didn't feel that I could master anything.

Then it happened. I was walking along one of the narrow streets in the 5th arrondissement, not far from Bang's place. I spotted an Algerian bar and felt compelled to go inside. It was one of those bars that once had been so plentiful on the left bank of the Seine but which had now been replaced by more fashionable bistros and shops. Dimly lit, Arabian music, primitive furniture and a smell of incense, shish kebab and cannabis. I could barely make out a row of smiling, white teeth in the darkness behind the bar and ordered a pastis. When my eyes got used to the poor light, I spotted him. In the mirror behind the bar I saw him sitting at one of the tables. The Seer. I turned around. The room was empty, and so was the mirror. But it was this unmistakable smile. I sipped my pastis and closed my eyes. Then I realized that there was something about this bar that belonged to a past era and another place. I saw something that looked like a bazaar with a large square. I knew that it was somewhere in Spain. I went out into the scorching heat and the piercing sunlight. The street was swarming with people, but my attention was caught by two men in deep conversation in the square. There was something disturbingly familiar about them. They seemed to be totally preoccupied with each other. I went closer until I could hear their voices, and although I did not understand the language they were speaking, I could use my eyes. I became aware that one was the learned one and the other was an itinerant singer. The learned one had a fair complexion and blue eyes. The singer was dark and had brown eyes. Suddenly, the singer looked in my direction. The other had also spotted me. At first they seemed surprised but then they smiled. The dark one lifted his arm as if he wanted to wave me over, but the learned one stopped him. Something in his eyes made me turn around. I started running. In and out between traders, snake charmers and fortune-tellers. A door slammed when I returned to the bar. I opened my eyes. A man with a dark complexion had let the door slam behind him and he disappeared behind the counter and into a back room. I drank my pastis and paid for it. I still had an hour before my train would leave from Gare du Austerlitz.

The wind had died down and it had stopped raining. I had been awake many times during the night but had apparently dropped off again since I woke up when someone called me. When I opened my eyes the Seer was in the doorway.

'What time is it?' I asked, a bit confused, and reached for my shirt.

'A few hours past elegance or five minutes before silliness. It's all up to you.'

I got up. He had boiled some water and put bread on the table while I had my shower. He watched me while I had my breakfast.

'If you want to be in touch with reality you must know

what real timing is. If you know that, you'll always be on time. Not five minutes before or five minutes past, but the exact moment where any given situation will have the best possible chance of success.'

He poured hot water into my cup and pushed the jar with instant coffee across the table.

'The time has come for you to replace the theories with practice. Try to watch one of your thoughts. Apparently, it rises out of nothing, and before you know it another has taken its place. It happens, and you can't do anything about it. If your "I" is also a thought, who is thinking then?'

The question was vibrating between us.

'When you have experienced your "I" dissolving, who was it that experienced this?'

Suddenly I was wide awake since these were questions I had asked myself many times without getting the slightest bit closer to an answer.

'That is why we have to move away from the level of behaviourism. We cannot deny the "self". But we must understand that there is a "self" that solely relates to the world, and another, higher "Self" which is without limitations and in perfect balance with all the aspects of life. While the little "self" is busy counting its money and planning the future, creating strategies and nurturing its career, shopping and consuming, worrying and looking for confirmation, the higher "Self" is simply concerned with *being*. While the little "self" feels that it needs all its activities in order to function, the higher "Self" *is*, because it is totally free of any excess luggage. That is why people sometimes experience that there are two different worlds. Such an experience, of course, is a beginning, but you should have passed that stage long ago. When you lose your timing it is simply because you aren't present. Most people think that if they really apply themselves and concentrate to the point of exhaustion, then they've got it. But it is really the other way round. You first have to loosen up and let go. You must be willing to let things be and to leave opportunities alone. No matter how obvious they may be. Then you must learn to sharpen your attention without any effort. This way you'll train your ability to be really present. Such presence is an extension of a deeper intuition. Do not confuse this with the traditional understanding of female intuition. The real intuition is more like a kind of omnipresence and omniscience, if you like. It is because of the certainty that this "Self" is able to *be*.'

'What kind of knowledge is this? What is really the point?'

'If we only relate to the level of behaviour, we soon find that everything we do and everything we seek is based on fear. As long as we remain at this level and refuse to see that there are other levels, we shall basically think and act from fear for the rest of our lives. This fear is based on the little self's knowledge that there isn't enough of anything for everybody, that it will be burgled if it doesn't hide behind thick walls and is insured against every kind of threat, that war shall break out if we do not rearm, and so on. The knowledge of the true Self is based on trust. It knows that its origin is universal. Since it is not interested in property or status, there is nothing to lose. The true Self knows where it comes from, why it is here and where it is going. When you forget this knowledge in all the commotion, you may only regain it by giving up everything the little self appreciates and adores.'

The words organized themselves in order like the cards in a game of solitaire, which had just worked out. I still sensed that he had left something out. That there was more behind the sentences. Something deeper, something, which might be so decisive and irrevocable that it neither ought nor could be said.

It cannot be said in any simpler way than in Shakespeare's immortal words: 'To be or not to be, that is the question.'

Unfortunately, these words have lost their power as time has gone by, and we have forgotten what they really mean.

He got up, indicating that it was time to go. Outside, the sun had now climbed over the mountaintop. The wet earth began to steam, and it looked as if it was going to be a clear day. On the slope workers had almost finished laying tiles on the roof of a building. Two cats were licking a ray of sunshine that fell on them. There was a golden glow over the town.

'It seems like a good day for flying,' the Seer said as he swung the car between the bushes and into the parking place.

We walked through the bramble. The sense of dissolving that I had felt the previous days, I now experienced as a natural and neutral state, which appeared the moment I whispered the word isogynic. We walked directly into the middle of Prat's meadow and the Seer turned towards me and asked:

'Who are you?'

The question was direct and surprised me. I hesitated. I had lulled myself into what I thought was a pure and neutral state, but realized right away that it was more an expression of a lack of responsibility, telling me that I was not really present. My mind was spinning. One concept followed another, but I could not decide which one would be appropriate here. How did I want to look? Who did I want to be? And while I was worrying about that I realized, this was exactly the reason that I, in relation to his question, was exactly as far off as I had been when he woke me up in the morning. I could now see all the pretentious notions I had had about myself. All the masks I had been hiding behind passed me by on an inner screen, like a film running off its reel at high speed. Then just the white light from the projector. Nothing! He didn't wait for my answer but continued:

'What do you want here?'

I knew that if my answer was 'nothing' it wouldn't be true and he would know it. I was also aware that he didn't ask the question in order to get an answer. He knew them already. It was just a way to help me sharpen my alertness. Everything happened so fast. I noticed how my ability to think clearly came to life through his intervention. Everything happened without delay and easily in his presence. Before I was able to find an answer I realized that they were all connected to the kind of basic fear he had mentioned earlier. There was nothing to add.

We began the ascent. I walked determinedly, leaning forward and jabbing my cane into the sand over the first, straight, steep stretch. The Seer walked upright with a light step, carrying his cane over his shoulder. The moment I saw that, I was immediately aware that this was part of his purpose, and that he wanted to show me that it was all a matter of attitude on both the physical, mental and spiritual levels. It was his way of telling me to straighten up and to regain my dignity. There was no reason to make it more difficult than necessary.

I straightened up and right away felt the agility of my back. We passed the first ledge. The air was bright and space was endless. The sun shone directly on the mountainside. The Seer was again in the lead and increased his speed. Once again I saw only the heels of his boots. Left, right, left, right. I was sweating and not till later did I notice that I had lost my posture. When we reached the second ledge I was not focused anymore, and ascending towards the third ledge, all of a sudden a series of thoughts appeared and I knew that they must come from him. *Illness comes from resistance! Resistance to change!* Above the abyss the eagle soared. It was now difficult for me to keep up. My breath was short and gasping, my legs heavy as lead. I took off my jacket and slung it over my shoulder. When we reached the fourth ledge I was convinced that he would stop. I had reached the end of my tether. But he continued without a word. He was now more than 10 metres ahead of me and I only continued because

I didn't want him to witness me throwing in the towel. In principle he could have been my father.

The path wound its way up and up and in and out between bushes and rocks, and suddenly he was out of sight. I hurried along the best I could. *Give up your resistance!* I partly crawled and partly walked. He was still out of sight when I turned the corner where he had disappeared. I went on. My lungs felt like a pair of bellows filled with sand. When finally I passed a section of the path full of bushes I saw him waiting further up. This gave me a new strength. He was standing at the edge of the ledge. I approached slowly. My legs gave way under me. All was quiet. Silent. I only felt the sense of floating that I had felt earlier at Prat des crémats. '*Come on!*' He called me over to the edge. I was no longer in control of my movements. Something came up from deep down in my memory. I could now see the abyss. I had a sinking feeling. An enormous chasm lay before me and somewhere in the dark I sensed my panic. *Let go now.* The voice was calm and precise. I was standing right at the edge. *I am with you.* My stomach contracted. *Show me your true Self.* He took my hand. *Now!* I closed my eyes and took one step forward. My hand squeezed his. It was like two electric leads touching. Like two flames freed from wax and wick, merging into one.

The flame burned with a bright glow in the clear, blue air. *Floating. Two persons on the ledge. The silver thread connecting us to ourselves. Endless rows of ideas and words like dominoes tumbling over one by one and burning in the air as far as one can see. Read them yourself.*

I opened my eyes and saw that I was standing one step away from the abyss.

'What was that?'

He smiled. But not his usual smile. He was very clear and glowing. The sight of him made my question completely meaningless. He had also taken off his jacket. I could see beads of sweat on his forehead. He seemed somehow changed, or maybe it was my way of looking at everything that had changed. There was now a totally different basal tone resonating. It was purer. Filled with a new kind of humour, far beyond puns and permissiveness. There was no longer a distance between us. In a split second two flames became one. The climb had been fierce and strenuous. The transference itself undramatic, quiet and easy. Everything I myself had pondered over, everything that had almost developed into a kind of existential pastime or a convenient hiding place, everything that I hitherto had understood on an intellectual and emotional level, was only a shadow of the reality he had just shown me. It had all just taken a short moment. Now I also knew that in each and every one of us there is more than one alternative. That we do have a choice and that we must be willing to make that choice. That immediately next to the fearful and the worried, the unhappy and the hateful, the self-asserting and the fraudulent, the envious and the greedy, there is always another kind of being, undivided and embracing, uncomplicated and whole. A flame, which will always burn, be it ever so small and thus placed in the remotest nook.

The Seer walked ahead of me on the way down. I couldn't help watching him. His relaxed ease filled with presence and care. Never before had I met anyone like him. He was of another world. But still there was something about him, which was very familiar. I was contemplating the thought that he had suddenly entered my life at a time where everything was black and disintegrating. If this was not an example of perfect timing, what kind of divine intervention might then be responsible? Why me? Why this mountain?

We made a short break on a ledge further down. We looked at the valley and the mountain in silence. This enormous, breathtaking and inexplicable view, which constantly found new ways of surprising me.

We arrived in town in time for a visit to the small, local bookstore *Libraire 'Le Gaulois'*, which stood facing the street. The owner, Thierry Salles, served wine since it was the last shopping day of the season. The small room was filled with books. I walked over to a shelf and pulled out a book. *Massacre at Montségur* by Zoé Oldenbourg. On the slope the workers were putting their tools away. Outside one of the houses an elderly woman was taking her laundry in from an unsteady clothes rack. The sun brushed its long and golden rays across the Pyrenees. The three of us standing on the street watched it disappear. Somewhere nearby a child laughed. I just stood there and felt that life was benign.

The night train for Madrid left Paris at 7.45 pm. I had entered the wrong carriage and was moving through the train in order to find the right one. The curtains were drawn in my compartment. I opened the door and stepped inside. A thin man sat squeezed into a corner. He was wearing a Nike T-shirt, a pair of thin, stained, gabardine trousers and a short imitation-leather jacket. I nodded and placed my suitcase on the floor between the seats. A sign on the wall told us that we were not allowed to pull out the cots. The staff would come and do that at 10 pm. I sat down diagonally opposite the thin man. He was in his mid 30s and undernourished. The greasy hair and the stubble told their own story. It was clear that he was not Spanish and did not look French either. He was fumbling with his bag placed on the seat next to him. When finally the zipper gave in, the compartment filled with the spicy smell of salami. He was rummaging in the bag and finally found what he was looking for. He placed a whole bottle of vodka on the small table by the window.

'From Ukraine,' he said in broken English. 'You want?'

My first thought was to decline his offer, but there was something about him, which made it difficult. I nodded hesitatingly. He was already emptying the sealed cup for brushing your teeth, which was filled with disinfected water, so that it might be used for the vodka. I protested when he filled it with vodka, but he cut me short with a: 'Vodka from the Ukraine, best in the world.'

He emptied yet another cup and filled it with vodka.

'Ukrainian vodka much better than Russian vodka. Russian vodka very bad.'

He raised his cup and touched mine. He emptied his at a single draught. I was sipping mine.

'Drink, drink,' he said elated.

He filled his cup once more. His movements and his whole demeanour told me that he had a problem. I took a bigger draught in a failed attempt to be polite, which made me cough it all up again.

'Drink, drink!' he yelled.

Although he was smiling, I could tell from his glassy stare that this was not a happy man.

'Where are you going?' I asked him.

'Madrid. Last week I go from Ukraine. I go Germany, I go Paris. Paris I stay two days. Now I go Madrid. Friend have bar in Madrid. He rich.'

I couldn't help wondering how he had managed in Paris for two days at this time of year. He didn't look as if he could afford a hotel. On the other hand, I wouldn't embarrass him by asking.

'Ukraine and Europe, friend – yes!'

He lifted his cup and emptied it. The effect was showing now. He leaned slantingly towards me:

'Europe kaput. Black people no good. Everywhere black people and Asian people. No good.'

The corners of his mouth now drooped condescendingly, under-lining his scorn.

'Ukraine and Europe, good, yes. White people, good, yes!'

He could hardly control his movements as he poured himself another drink. Time dragged heavily by. He poured, we lifted our cups. I tried to make my sips look convincing, but it really didn't matter anymore. He didn't take any notice but became more and more angry with the world, which he blamed for the misery that had befallen the country he came from. If someone had offered him an armband with a swastika it would probably not cost them more than a glass of vodka. It was very difficult to like him. Suddenly I could see him. I could look through the layers of loss, abuse, pain, inferiority and hatred. It didn't take a degree in psychology to see that. But there was something else as well.

He is five years old. Together with his smaller sister he is bending over his mother, who is on the floor in an awkward position. They are trying to wake her up. Later, the neighbour comes in to help, but the mother doesn't wake up. He is walking along the main street in the village where he used to live many years ago. There are no other people in the street. All the houses are empty. There is a grey light all over. In an enclosure a few cars are parked in front of a grey building. Power plant. He walks to the other end of the village. He is standing in front of a garden gate leading up to a big, dilapidated wooden house. Orphanage. Night-time. He is running towards a tall fence. Factory. A dog is chasing him. Behind him a guard in a pool of blood. The spoils do not even come to half a day's wages. He is walking along a street in a city. It is cold and people are busy. At a square, where you can buy anything, he is exchanging his warm overcoat for a posh leather jacket that will make him look more respectable in Europe.

When the steward came to prepare for the night he was already sleeping heavily. His head had sunk onto his chest and he was drooling. The cup was turned over and a small river of vodka was running across the floor. I wiped his face, got the jacket off him and managed to get him to bed. As I tugged the blanket around him, he opened his eyes and mumbled:

'Ukraine, best place in the world.'

Far into the darkness I saw a light. The flame was not very clear, but it was there.

7

Day by day we worked our way closer and closer to the top of the mountain. At the same time the Seer helped me to get further and further past the edge of the conceivable. We repeated the same steps every day, and I felt my ability to focus and to concentrate getting better and the feeling of being present intensifying. As the days went by it became clear, that everything he did had a higher purpose and was part of a larger plan. Together with him life became an instrument of change where we were playing on all its keys. It was a symphonic process of cleansing and realization. As he put it:

'How can you move if you are not willing to let go of everything that blocks the way? Man is an instrument that has to be tuned in order to play in tune.'

When he thought that a day had passed particularly well we celebrated with Gilbert at the Costes. We were dancing on the ruins of all the miseries that had been laid to rest that day, so to speak. This was a way of showing our respect for every single item that had now served its purpose.

The evening prior to the last workday we set the table in the banqueting hall and lit a fire. I prepared a simple meal. The Seer put a bottle of Don Cesar on the table. Outside, it had started to rain again. Gusts of wind made the shutters bang against the window frames.

'We have actually finished this round. You have found the way. But this is only a beginning. A totally new way of life is beginning for you here. As I told you on the first day, life will not necessarily become easier from now on. But you will now know why the problems arise and you will have the tools to overcome them if that is what you want. Tomorrow we shall ascend all the way to the fortress. There are no more tests for you. You are just going to see what is ahead. *The Shaft of the Soul*, the Gate of Time and the Grail. Consider this the crowning glory of the work you have done until now.'

It was a sad feeling that I was going to leave him and this place. Never before had I felt such intense meaning in life. Probably because I had met a man who dared take it seriously. He changed the fragmented and the physical into unity and spirit. Life was movement. A fairy tale. He showed me that there was a way, a purpose and a way to fulfil it. He lifted his glass:

'Let us toast the Norns. Here's to Urd, Verdande and Skuld. They have been your guardian angels here. They did a good job.'

The wind came up, became powerful and whispered through doors and cracks. The shadows danced a final dance in the banqueting hall by the light of the flickering candles and the flames from the open fireplace. Peace was beyond time.

The train arrived at Madrid Chamartin just before nine a.m. Nikolai looked even more pale and ill in the glaring sunlight on the platform. He looked around slightly confused as if he expected to be met by someone, and stalled a bit when we parted. I watched him as he disappeared in the crowd. I then spent half an hour looking for the tube for Atocha, from where I was to continue by train to Malaga. I could already smell the scent of my Spain. This strange conglomerate of a country, which had made me return again and again since I set foot here for the first time 25 years ago.

Breakfast at Atocha Renfe. Fried eggs and toast. Bustle and light. Conversation with a young, Italian girl who asks me if I can spare a bit of money for a cup of coffee. She is on her way to Seville to try her luck as a dancer. Big smile on the surface. Sad and lonely. Tells me that Italy is no-future. Rootless and restless and far too young to be an existential refugee. Offer her breakfast and moral support.

Did we recognize each other because we were both refugees? What kind of future did she expect to find there, that she couldn't find anywhere else? I then remembered Itálica to the north of Seville, the first town that the Romans established in Spain. Here they built the biggest amphitheatre outside of Rome. This was the spot where the gladiator fights had become so cruel, that Marcus Aurelius finally banned them. *Those who are about to die — salute you!* This was the way that gladiators saluted emperors and consuls before going into battle. She waved and smiled valiantly as she disappeared in the direction of Seville. A quarter past 12, I started the final lap of the journey.

The wind had died down and it had stopped raining. Instead, the fog thickened in the valley. Walking through the thicket the certainty of the natural condition was underlined. No worries, no trouble. In the meadow he asked me to walk out to meet Prat alone. She was already waiting. *Here is a square. Walk into each of the corners and give each one a quality. Then collect them into your own force in the middle. One by one they came from the upper right corner and moved clockwise. Care. Strength. Courage. Compassion. They dissolved in one single movement and met in a single point: Silence!*

We walked side by side along the first, difficult part. I walked with my cane across my shoulder and walked with a light step. We moved slowly upwards. I walked ahead. I turned around on the first ledge. Although I was slowly getting used to this it still took me by surprise that he was gone. I was going up alone.

The air was full of oracles. *A man is walking along a long road. He is lost. He gets very happy when he meets another human being.* The Norns were there. The visions floated in and out of the fog. *An encouraging word doesn't cost much, and the price of a little support doesn't necessarily have to be high.* I walked empty-handed through the void and was filled up.

They were everywhere. They made the trees and the bushes come alive. Each and every pebble on the path became a star in the universe. I knew every turn and every boulder. My breath fell into harmony with the shape of the mountain. Point by point and ledge by ledge I moved upwards with ease.

I had passed all the well-known places. The path grew narrower towards the end and seemed more and more like a maze. Pulling free of the thicket I got a glimpse of the fortress through the fog. The Seer stood waiting outside of it. This was how it had to be.

'Perfect,' he said – 'Perfect.'

His words struck a chord, clear as a bell, in my mind.

'I'm now going to show you *The Shaft of the Soul*. The bridge between life and death. On the walls of that shaft you'll see many pictures from your own life. Once in a while you'll see a dark square. One day, when you become familiar with this condition, you may go in and exchange the dark square with a window. You may then open it and make it golden. Walk through it and push your way further and further in. But today I'll only show you the shaft to give you an indication of what it is. Stand there.'

I stepped in front of him. It lasted a moment only and was totally undramatic.

I am standing in a tube with nondescript walls. Many pictures of situations, people and places are seen in one single, indescribable picture. There is a golden light streaming down from above. It has no shape. All the places are one place. All pictures are one picture. All persons are one person. I rush upwards through the shaft at top speed and get born with a sound like a cork being pulled out of a bottle.

The Norns had put out water and biscuits for us. I was watching the fortress. It wasn't very big. It seemed quite impossible that 205 people should have lived here for a longer period of time. He got up and called me to the gate of the fortress.

'This is the gate of time. You must stand in it.'

I did as he told me.

'This is the shapeless opening where all of time becomes eternity. The past, the present and the future all become one. There is no division.

'Everything *is* in the same moment. If you become accepting, then you will always be the person you were supposed to be.'

The tone vibrated. The reverberation mixed with the silence and became endless, it was like an echo of the one moment that contained everything. *You were not caught by time, it was you who dissolved it.*' I stepped into the courtyard. It was almost pentagonal. There was an unreal atmosphere, which was enhanced by the dense fog. Something drew me into the middle of the courtyard. I was facing the tower, which

The Gate of Time: The Castle seen from The Castle

was situated to the north. To my left the gate of time through which I had just passed. Opposite, to my right, a smaller gate opened to the east. I wanted to see what was on the other side, but I couldn't move. I was held firmly to the spot by an inexplicable power. Any kind of resistance was unimaginable. I gave up my thoughts and remained quiet.

While I was standing like this a veiled woman came through the big gate. She walked softly closer leaning slightly forward, as if she didn't want to disturb. She passed me closely by and looked at me from her awkward pose with an indefinable smile. She had no age. She greeted me silently, walking softly on and disappearing through the small gate. A short time after, another woman appeared from the fog and repeated the same pantomime, and after her yet another.

'Come closer.'

It was the Seer. I stepped forward.

'I'm now going to show you the Grail. Or rather its basic thought form. You will be able to see it and touch it, but it is up to you to see it in its variable form, which it has right now. But the basic form is always the same, and this is what you'll see in a little while. It is true that the Cathars possessed it. No one managed to take it from them, since it did not exist as a physical thing, it was pure spirit. A higher form of consciousness.'

He held both his arms in front of him as if he wanted to conjure up something or other from the earth. He guided my hand to the same place in the air where he had just formed the invisible sculpture. There were no words, just a confirmation. '*You can do it. Do it!*'

Standing like this we suddenly heard female voices singing. In a corner of the fortress the three women from before were holding each other's hands. More human shapes appeared from the fog. A small group of five tourists wearing macs and cameras. The Norns waved me closer. We all took each other's hands. Then we began singing:

The Grail in its fundamental thoughtform as seen by The Seer

'O *Signore, fati me, un instrumentum, della tua pacem.*'

The voices fused into a tone, which had been struck ages ago. I recognized the words from the prayer of St Francis of Assisi. The Seer was standing in the middle of the courtyard. Around him a weak fluorescent light was visible. We stood still and listened in silence to the tune that surrounded the fortress, as the song ebbed away. What had made us come here? As we introduced ourselves to each other it struck me. One woman was from Romania, one from Sweden and one from England. One man was Jewish and from the USA, the last one was from Italy. They all worked in Brussels. I looked at the Seer. He was standing in the fog in front of the gate of time smiling inscrutably.

In the evening we drove to Villeneuve D'Olme to dine at 'Le Castrum', far outside of Ariége, well known for its food and good service. Here as well, the Seer was welcomed like royalty. We were the only guests. We were placed at a lavishly set table in the middle of the room. Behind the Seer a young and beautiful waitress was standing. Behind me her twin brother. Opening the menu the head waiter signalled the two, and, as if conjured out of nothing, they poured the wine we had ordered. The three of them worked in the same rhythm. Not one unnecessary movement, everything fully co-ordinated and in tune with each other. They anticipated every wish and fulfilled them almost before we had had the thought ourselves.

'I love to come here. It is a study of timing and precision that one can never grow tired of.'

The Seer nodded approvingly towards the beautiful woman as she served the first course. When she leaned over to pour the wine, he whispered a gallant aside, which made her blush. He turned to me and said:

'From now on you must practise becoming invisible. That way you'll get rid of the last remnants of old traumas that you didn't remove here. Try as much as possible to avoid publicity. Do not waste too much attention on the world but go into your inner sanctity and prepare yourself there. You must sharpen your precision and your timing. You must learn to fall into the cosmic flow of life. Concentration is not the same as attention. Concentration separates and excludes. Attention sees everything as one, without any resistance or reservation. Instinct is not the same as intuition. And intuition is not the same as *intuition*! When you get home, things will begin to happen. Do not despair when you find that worldly opportunities pass you by. Remember the old saying that if you think only one single, noble and unselfish thought in a mountain cave, then it will form vibrations throughout the universe and will do what must and can be done.'

He raised his glass. There were so many things I wanted to ask him.

'But how am I to integrate everything you showed me. How do I use it in my everyday life?'

'Don't worry about that. It will all merge into a higher synthesis.'

We raised our glasses and it was time for the main course. The Seer was at his best. The flirtation he had started with the young girl developed into a dance with their eyes, hidden movements, a well-chosen word and an accidental touch, all the time balancing between innocence and sensuality. It was breathtakingly beautiful to watch his virtuosity in showing her his appreciation without it ever becoming awkward. On the contrary, it placed the moment in a beautiful perspective. Lifted it out of timeliness. Her eyes were radiant and her movements became more and more graceful. Everything had gained a new meaning. Everything was exactly as it was supposed to be.

Suddenly something flew through the air. I got a shock. It all happened so fast. One single movement. Across the table and without toppling one single glass. It was the Seer. To this day I do not know how it was done, but suddenly he was standing next to me with a forefinger against my chest.

'Allow me to remind you of the things I have taught you. Be vigilant. Dance! Also when you are sitting down quietly. Be present. Here! Now!'

Before I had collected myself he was again sitting in his own seat. Behind him the woman had difficulty keeping her composure. He said a few words to her in his usual, elegant way. Then she couldn't hold back anymore and broke into uncontrollable laughter. This started an avalanche. In one split second all behaviour exploded and everything dissolved into laughter. But as if by magic all went back to normal. The waiters disappeared and shortly after they returned and served the dessert. The Seer raised his glass:

'Come back to Andalusia next year, and we shall begin the real work!'

The next morning he drove me to Foix. We drank a pastis in a bar in the town square. We were both silent. We shook hands outside the train station. I wanted to say something, mumbled a thankyou but couldn't really find any other words.

'See you in Spain,' he said.

He then turned around and walked towards the town without looking back.

Sitting in the train heading for home and looking in my bag for my diary I found an envelope. I opened it and found a large silver ring inside it. Something was engraved on it. '*Crede Et Vicisti.*' Inside the ring, my name.

Home again, life became just as difficult as the Seer had predicted. After a series of nocturnal dreams which culminated in a dream taking place in a baronial castle, where I acknowledge that I am who I am, I am handed a hand-woven rug by a caliph. It is embroidered with Arabic letters telling me that I have passed the exam.

After this dream I felt totally out of touch with my old reality. Over and over again I had to remind myself of the inscription of the ring, 'believe and you'll win'. Instead of getting closer to the world, I felt that the distance had grown. I was back in a vacuum. My financial situation was still in shambles. All my extrovert, work-related activities failed. Only when I walked into the forest did the world become whole again. Once in a while I experienced the basic simplicity so intensely that I stayed there all day long. I would sit with my back against the trunk of a tree at the edge of the forest facing the beach and listen to the sea and watch the clouds slowly drifting across the sky. I then began to understand what deep layers the Seer had opened in me. I began to understand that the time of the trees, the sea and the clouds were that of the rhythm of the heart and the breath and totally in contrast with the kind of time-frame that man normally uses. I could just *be*. But could I live with that? It seemed like an insoluble paradox until the day I finally remembered:

'You are not going to live from it. You are going to *be* it and to write about it.' That was what he had said.

'Thus shall everything fall into place. What must happen will happen.'

When, a few weeks later, I was heading a three-day workshop about the creative process for songwriters and composers, I experienced for the first time a new level that I had brought with me from Montségur. On the last day of the workshop, whilst I was writing comments for each of the participants in my hotel room, I suddenly received some inexplicable pictures in my head, and I immediately wrote them down. I told the team on the following day that I wasn't quite sure what these pictures meant, and that they should disregard them if they didn't make any sense. However, if they did, I would certainly like to know. It turned out that some of the pictures and some of the comments were so precise that they went straight to the core of the personal space of the particular individual.

The inspiration from the presence of the Seer's personality was unmistakable. I felt that he wanted to show me, when you are willing to set yourself and your own wishes aside, you may then become a flawless mirror for other people. I myself experienced that I could see the participants in a clear light, devoid of any kind of assessment or judgement. Teacher or student, what difference did it make?

I also felt his inspiration in my everyday life. During the months leading up to my 50th birthday I started to have nocturnal dreams, which apparently had something to do with my past. The dreams were so intense that each affected me for several days. In the beginning I didn't understand what they tried to tell me. But then I woke up one morning after having dreamt about meeting the Seer in one of them.

'Acknowledge your mistakes,' he said with his familiar smile.

'I thought that was done at Montségur,' I objected.

'Well, apparently that wasn't enough.'

He spoke directly to my conscience. I then understood that just like that time on Montségur I had to relate directly to his words. But for how long should this cleansing continue?

'As long as it takes,' I heard him saying.

'Be willing always to unmask the motives of the little self. That is the only way to deal with them.'

In the following days I searched my memory for unconsidered episodes and actions in my life, which until now had been veiled in the darkness of oblivion. I wrote everything down as it appeared. Page after page of situations where I had hurt someone or had acted on the basis of my own, selfish needs. All my lies. Black and white. The little 'innocent' theft many years ago. The smarting remark. The unsympathetic attitude. The unworthy manipulations. Women. Everything. It was shocking how much I could still find in the nooks and crannies of my mind and which I had ignored or repressed with a shrug of the shoulders as time went by. I now had to relate to everything once again. It was not just embarrassing it was an inevitable, naked pain.

A large part of a whole life's correspondence – notes, scraps of paper, photographs and so on – was put into cardboard boxes. It wasn't your regular birthday party. Instead I started a bonfire in the garden. At exactly 12 noon my shabby and glorious past went up in flames.

'Are you sure about this?' asked one of my friends who happened by.

'Apart from this,' I replied, 'I'm not sure of anything at all.'

On the same day I received a letter headed 25 Gammel Kongevej September 26th, 1905:

'Dear . . .

No, I'm sorry, I cannot offer the service of reciting anything any more. The curtain has come down — the Iron Curtain. It is so sad not to be able to help any longer. But it is over.

Many kind regards

Herman Bang.'

Bang was 51 when he wrote this letter. I read the lines over and over. The well-known, spidery writing stood out on the paper and became legible.

He is sitting at the window looking at St Joergen's lake across the road. There is a wind coming up. Why write anymore? Here? Dizzy. On his hand a stain of soya which he removes with some difficulty. The truth? The stain of shame on the heart cannot be removed. Travel. Yes, travel. Away. Forever. Being nothing at all. A tired fly buzzes in the otherwise so quiet rooms at Gammel Kongevej 99 years ago.

It was an ice-cold day in February. The kind of day where

Copenhagen Central Station is anything but inviting. I dragged my suitcases up the stairs to get out of the chilling wind from the platform and quite deliberately ignored the beggars and the down-and-outs squatting on old newspapers and waving their blue coffee-pots at the passers-by. My own budget was more than over the limit, and, furthermore, I felt dizzy. I felt nauseated. I wasn't myself at all. Had I misunderstood something, since I could lose my balance to such a frightening degree? And just now, when I was about to embark on what was probably the most important journey of my life.

8

The rails sang as the train rushed into a curve at high speed
and disappeared into the darkness. I was dozing off but woke
up for a minute as my head hit the window. The afternoon
sun flickered into the compartment shortly after. We had left
Sierra de Almijara and were on the last straight lap towards
Malaga. Forty-eight hours of travelling were coming to an
end. I was now embarking on another kind of travel. I closed
my eyes and sank into the rocking movement of the train.
Into the wordless language. Into the black hole of memory.
Into Patio de los Leones. Into the singer who for the first
time leaned against the pillars at the courtyard of the Lions at
Alhambra in Granada in order to let himself be perpetuated
there, and without any hesitation lead the photographer
through to the residence of the emperor. Into the reception
room Mexuar. Into the Myrtle garden and his beloved Sala

de los Embajadores. What had made me go to Spain at that time? What was it that kept drawing me there? Behind it all I seemed to see a glimpse of the Seer and his familiar smile as a watermark on the veil that was slowly being withdrawn. A dying summer bee on a windowsill. A buzzing fly in an apartment on Gammel Kongevej. The *Old* King's Road? *King of* ... what? An ephemeral person on his way out of showbiz? *Store* Kongensgade. The Grand King's road. Alhambra and Montségur. Memory. Apparently, it was no coincidence that the lines seemed to meet in Andalusia in order to be transformed into the invisible red thread of their own history. What kind of manuscript was it? Who wrote it and where was it hidden?

The three-dimensional papier-mâché reproduction of Picasso's *Guernica* was still hanging over the descent to the coastal railway, exactly the way it did when I was here the last time. The Seer waited at the bar under one of the surrealists' invisible clocks at the far end of the train station.

'Well, have you regained your elegance?' he asked smilingly, as if he wanted to indicate that time was not operating here.

I looked at him, slightly puzzled, and was about to ask him what he meant.

'The Central Station in Copenhagen,' he continued.

'Oh,' I replied, and stood on one leg with open arms á la Edie Sedgewick.

I had happily forgotten all about dizziness and nausea. The electrical impulse in my spine. That had been a greeting from him then!

His car was parked outside. We drove along the coast on the motorway, which quite appropriately was nicknamed 'Death road'. I couldn't help thinking, what had made him settle down here in the middle of a touristy cesspool of deep-frying smells, plastic and concrete slum. I didn't ask him.

'I live in Switzerland. I live in Italy. I live in Alpha

Centauri. Omega Centauri. What difference does it make? I live everywhere and nowhere. Right now, I am living here. Let me tell you something. Years ago I met a man who had been in jail for 10 years. In order not to lose his mind while inside, he began studying. He read everything he could put his hands on, all the philosophers, works of natural science, the old religious scriptures, simply everything. I think he also took a degree in philosophy. At the same time he kept a strict account of the days, the weeks, the months and the years. He was convinced that the world would have changed when he re-entered society. When finally the day arrived and he impatiently walked out of the prison gate in his own suit, he experienced that the expected feeling of freedom failed to come. Several weeks of partying didn't change anything. He simply realized that his idea of freedom had been linked to an illusory idea of "freedom" being outside the prison walls, and "imprisonment" inside. He could go wherever he wanted. But on another level he was still a prisoner and a slave of his own expectations and those of others, of the prejudices, imaginings, habits, dreams and desires. Even 10 years of studying all forms of knowledge did not change the simple fact that he did not feel in the least free.'

He left the motorway.

The house was situated in a square in the old part of town. The church bells were tolling for evensong. The sun disappeared behind the houses and the guests in front of the cafes went inside. A boy on a moped without a silencer was circling the square with a girl sitting behind him. The one-legged, lottery vendor looked at himself in the reflection of the fountain and got ready to pack up, while the horns of the cars gave a concert in the main street under the haze of petrol. A beautiful, mature *doña* dressed in black greeted the Seer as we crossed the square. The balconies were overflowing with blazing geraniums. He lifted his white straw hat. A soft wind in an old figtree. The entrance was halfway down Don Quixote. We took the elevator to the fifth floor. There were five rooms in the apartment. It was furnished in a simple style. A view of the town and the Mediterranean. I unpacked my suitcase in the guest room and prepared the tape recorder. We had water and a single pastis on the terrace facing the square. Ben Webster was playing. Everything was deeper and more clearly outlined. It was like coming home.

'We'll start tomorrow. We'll be busy in the next few days. When my telephone consultation hour finishes at 9 a.m. you'll see how I work and how the energies work. You may ask all the questions you need to ask after lunch. Similar to the days on Montségur we shall dissolve all limitations. Have you brought a crash helmet?'

It was dark as we went out for dinner. The streets were closely lined with restaurants. The waiters moved about restlessly. It was out of season. However, there was still a hint of nauseating sun-oil and the tourist's menu mixed with the smell of Mediterranean salt and desert wind. We had Chinese.

At exactly 8 a.m. the first client phoned. The door to the Seer's study was ajar. He listened, spoke a few words that I couldn't hear and then placed the receiver on his writing desk. I could now see the kind of silence I had experienced at the other end of the line and that I heard as a kind of white noise. He lifted his hand and let it hover over something that I couldn't identify. He sat like this for a long time. He then picked up the receiver, spoke a few words and hung up. They called from far and near. He spoke English then German, French then Italian. This continued for an hour. Every time he hung up it started ringing. I sneaked into the kitchen to prepare tea and toast. He looked tense coming out of the study. He was somewhere else. We ate our breakfast standing up.

'Something bothering you?' I asked.

The Seer at work in his study

'Well, an Italian ambassador had a stroke in the Far East. This was his wife. I told her that I couldn't go on repairing him this way. I first told him to retire many years ago, but he never wanted to listen. Each time he has a stroke, his wife calls me because it is faster than calling the emergency. But some day even I shall not be able to help him. He is holding on to life with his fingertips. If he falls this time there is no way back. I have already given him one treatment, but he needs another.'

I followed him into his study. He started right away. Lifted his hand and let it hover over his desk.

'What are you doing?' I asked.

'I am visualizing a picture of him and then sending it the relevant energies. I can see that one of his heart valves doesn't function properly. His blood circulation isn't very good either. I now check all the other organs and I see that something is wrong with his digestion. All in all, he is not in balance. It looks as if he needs the whole package. Organs, blood circulation, chakras and aura. Follow me.'

He signalled to me that I should be quiet. The grail sculpture was on the desk in front of him refracting the light. I concentrated and tried to sense his reality. He wasn't there. He was looking far into the distance. His eyes saw something that others couldn't see. The galaxies moved through unknown universes. I sat completely still with a straight back. I thought I saw something like very small glimpses of light in the air. I felt electrical impulses. I closed my eyes.

Through a thin haze of grey light something bluish shone through at the edges.

A flame-like thought. The Seer is bending over a stoutly built man on a cot. He is working in deep concentration and very determined. The man's breathing is very poor. The light changes and turns blue. The Seer is taking one of the luminous particles in the air. It shines with a golden light like a star. He is placing the crystal where the heart used to be and closes.

'Îkhal!'

Complete. Activated. The reinstatement of the original condition. He blows on his hands and moves them over the sick body.

'Ephatah!' — *In one single instant he opens the man's blood circulation, the chakras and the aura. He then whispers something to the sleeping man. A long line unfolds and becomes endless. It is a whole life but it lasts a short while only.*

'Done!'

I opened my eyes. The Seer was standing up.

'Could you follow that?'

I was still shaken.

'It felt like eternity and yet like a single moment.'

'Well, we are working with powerful energies.'

He looked more relaxed now. He smiled relieved.

'Our friend can go another round. It might be the last one. I'm not so sure that there'll be another. And I told his wife. It is up to him.'

'What did you whisper to him?'

'I didn't whisper anything. If that is what you experienced it is because you were in the psychic or astral area. Since in this case I had no possibility of giving the client an option for his present situation by word of mouth, I transferred it directly with the healing itself. Hopefully, it is going to manifest and become expressed in another way of living and another attitude. But sometimes it is easier to move a rock than a human being. Even the gods fight in vain against this kind of inertia.'

He seemed to be surprised at the way I had experienced this.

'It's fine that you are able to see anything at the psychic/ astral level, but I'd like you to be able to see clearly. If this had been the case you would have seen the client's incarnation picture. You would then have seen that the cause for his present condition is spread out over a longer period of time than this single life. Furthermore, you would immediately have seen the connection between his poor heart and the star Rigel in the Orion constellation, and you would have known that this is where you had to seek help. You would have seen the connection between micro- and macro cosmos. When it is a matter of treating physical diseases it is an advantage to operate on the ethereal level. But it is still limited in itself. The astral level has a tendency to become flighty and is also limited. Both the astral and the mental level are more or less tied to the personal level. But there is a higher aspect of all three levels, a universal, creative area which dissolves all limitations. In order to see clearly it is absolutely necessary to be able to let go of everything that is connected to yourself. In such a condition there are no pictures as we normally understand the word. Instead of a linear, horizontal way of looking it is more of a circular, vertical concentration, which is immediate. You have a long way to go and you might as well start right away and properly. Tonight I'll show you a simple but effective exercise that you may use. I shall now take you to the Tolox Mountain. Later, we'll have lunch at the town of Tolox.

Tolox was situated about 50 kilometres into the mountains. For a long time it felt like driving in a virtual reality of cardboard stage-set wings with one hastily erected holiday apartment complex after the other, broken only by equally stereotypical and hastily built golf courses and hotels. Not until we got up further did the architectonic horrors change into citrus groves and blooming almond trees. The hairpin bends got tighter and the road more and more bumpy. We were at an altitude of 1800 metres and followed the last gravel road until it came to an end. He parked the car and we started climbing along the path. Similar to Montségur we went through the initiation points. So that I did not forget them, as he said! I sensed that this was about something else. We sat down further up. I unpacked my tape recorder and we got started on the questions of the day. When we finished we sat quietly and watched the endless view. I was slowly realizing that this was one of the Seer's qualities that I appreciated the most. To be present without words, without expectations and without any judgement. These were the times when I felt that he could communicate his thoughts and visions through his presence alone. Looking out became looking in. It was an undramatic kind of transmission, which would move you almost imperceptibly and silently. At these moments I felt my body relax completely. Each fibre, each muscle and every single cell found its correct place. An empathetic vigilance grew from this relaxed condition, a vigilance, which saw people and things as they were on their own merit. This was not about acceptance anymore, since there was nothing to accept. Everything was as it was. It was a long forgotten language. He showed me how almost all communication between people, the spoken and the written word, is nothing but our desperate attempts to cling to illusory personalities and identities tainted by prejudices, fear and vanity. A language which did not allow any room for listening, which focused on itself, which was excluding and only lived due to its attack and defence system was, according to him, a poor and inhumane one. Although the users of this language were usually very good at repartees and were able to write infinitely, they were really only good at maintaining and communicating limitations without end. It was this maintaining of limitations which was one of the main reasons that the great paradigm change, which all were waiting for, did not happen. He did not judge. He simply looked at and worked for the release of limitations wherever he met them. Not until the dissolution of all mental noise would it be possible to practise the transmission of stillness as a transforming kind of communication between people. It was not possible to enter this condition with a limited attention. The road to the transpersonal and the related level might seem difficult, because it demanded an obligation which included the complete human being. It was not enough to be just a little bit pregnant. You either were or you were not. And the paradoxical difference between the one and the other was the simple fact that the sleeping person decided to open his eyes, to wake up and become conscious of his wakeful condition. The fact that such a seemingly simple decision could appear so difficult lay in the fact that it entailed the release of more or less everything that you have ever learned and gained, and which you erroneously have interpreted as a true realization.

He presented all these considerations to me on the mountain. In one single thought, without words, without judgement.

On our way back to the car he suddenly stopped.

'Do you feel it?'

I stopped in my tracks. He pointed to the shadows in front of us and then into the distance. The Sun stood at an angle behind us. I looked at the horizon and then down the mountainside. Now I saw it. The shadows moved. The mountain moved. The earth moved. And we were standing on it. It was a magnificent experience. For one single moment I experienced that we were standing on a globe that moved forward majestically. Moving around a sun in a galaxy in the universe. The silence. The clouds. The grass. The shadows. The pulse. The breathing. Unity. Gravitation. The whisper of the universe in the wind.

'Quite moving, isn't it?' he said smiling.

We drove down to Tolox and had our siesta at the local *venta*. We continued working on our questions and answers after lunch. We then started talking about art and the role of the artist:

'When artists receive something from the universe they are

able to transform it into something beautiful. Not beautiful in the ordinary sense, but beautiful in a universal sense so that the power is expressed in work. But almost everyone is taken in by their egotism. Therefore art does not play the role it was meant to play. Artists are generally small children who like to play without understanding the power they are playing with. And the more art is personified the lesser-art it is. The artists, then, are no longer the mouthpiece of the universe. The gifts that are given to them are not given for their own sake.

A good writer, poet, painter, musician, filmmaker, singer or dancer is an interpreter of the universal language, the impressionable language, words, pictures and music that moves. It is not their inspiration, not a gift for their personalities, but something they are obligated to interpret and to pass on. Then it becomes beautiful. The Seer sees and – moves. The painter paints out of the universal, not out of himself and not for his own sake or for the sake of money. Leonardo da Vinci was formidable. He was able to transform things in the same spirit as he received them. He was the mouthpiece of visions. It was a kind of clear-sightedness. He understood that it was his task to develop a prophetic sense.

It was clear that he wanted to emphasize this.

'There is no true art apart from the ability to see and to listen at a super-sensitive level. To be receptive to cosmic impulses. An artist must be willing to sharpen his consciousness and his intuition in order to see and to liberate the humane and the cosmic in even the most insignificant, the banal, the superficial and the mediocre. He must never let himself sink to the level of simple reproduction. The task of the artist is transformation. Unfortunately, only very few are willing to give up their personal ambitions, their egotism, the strategies of which are always blocking the way to a higher realization.'

It grew dark before we got back to the apartment.

He placed a burning candle in front of me.

'This lesson moves us right back to the beginning. It is solely about concentration. Nothing else. Sit down in front of the candle. Relax and concentrate on your natural breathing. Do not force anything. Concentrate on all the stages of breathing in and breathing out; the short break between the breath's transition from the inner to the outer. Feel your coexistence with the world, with the universe. The energies which run through your breathing connecting you to the air and the atmosphere, the universe and the cosmos. Now, look at the flame and concentrate on the wick itself, then the visible light and finally the aura of heat that the flame radiates. Now, close your eyes and visualize these three dimensions of light in front of your inner eye. Bring the flame inside and let it lighten your innermost room. Feel how you are fused together. You are one. The flame is you and you are it. See how frail it is. The slightest breath of air may blow it out. But it should not be hidden under a bushel. Later, when you master this lesson, you may expand it and move to the beginning so to speak.'

He put his hands together and opened them shaping the wings of a butterfly.

'In this lesson, looking at the flame, you must at the same time consider the consciousness which is looking at the flame.'

I fell asleep with a thousand flames dancing in front of my eyes. Later, in a dream, they all became one.

9

'Ask your question through all the universes.'

The voice came from the flame. There was a face in it. A Greek philosopher. The face changed and took on Roman features. The wick in the flame disappeared. Only the pure flame remained. It had a totally golden and clear aura with a cool, blue centre. It was burning clearly in the air. A new face appeared. It was the Seer.

'Now you are present,' the voice said.

Then I woke up.

I got up and got ready for the task of the day, which started with an hour of stillness. The Seer was already seated in his consulting room. His eyes were only partly open. They didn't see anything. They saw everything. Outside a storm was brewing. A sunshade on a balcony on the opposite side of the street overturned and was being blown over the edge. I sat down in the living room and tried to find my way into an inner silence but was constantly disturbed by the noise from the street. Then I noticed one of the pictures on the wall. It was an old engraving depicting Marcus Aurelius. Next to it was a small painting. It showed the interior of a room in semidarkness. A person was dimly to be seen in one corner of the room. A vague notion made me stand up in order to study the picture more closely. Standing in front of it I could see that it was a picture of a Moorish building. Tiles decorated with braided ribbons made out of 12-pointed stars formed the friezes around the closed and arched windows. In between them was a door. Above it calligraphic, ornamental ribbons. The person in the corner seemed to be a woman dressed in a traditional dress with a veil. Memory.

The first client phoned at exactly eight a.m. Each time the connection was interrupted a new one called. I cleaned the kitchen and prepared breakfast so that it would be ready as soon as the Seer had finished the consultations of the day. He was bustling with energy as he sat on the kitchen table with a cup of coffee.

'Today I'll tell you about healing. When I talk about being willing to move out into the universe in order to find an answer, you must understand that man is himself a part of this universe. When you open yourself to the cosmic energies then we are dealing with a sort of dual attention. It is directed both inwards and outwards. Things are united. As it is inside, so is it outside. Physically, mentally and spiritually. When you obtain harmony with the universal laws you fulfil your purpose. It is an all-inclusive level where you cannot talk about the outer space without including the inner space. That which lies beyond man. When I heal I return freedom to the person in question. This is the case in all its simplicity. I try to remove the concept of power in a person. Remove the criteria for success, everything that is crippling to a human being. In

The Isogynic Being

this way I can, maybe, remove the diseases of the body and of the mind. But I must move in order to move others. I must be able to see the connections and the deeper meaning. Ask the question: "What can I do?" This way you make yourself available. Unlimited. This is the only true way in which to be present. It is the prerequisite to seeing. When you turn your back on the underlying reality then you turn your back on your finest qualities. When I see I can move – I then have a responsibility. When I do not see, then I'm irresponsible. We can ask any question of the stars and the galaxies and they will all answer us.

'It is sad when we do not use this potential. It is so essential, so simple that most people do not know what I'm talking about. But if man knew, if man only knew how things are connected and how much influence they have on their own destiny. Think – come on!'

The light crawled slowly across the wall behind him. The sounds from the street grew faint and disappeared between the words.

'It might be that as a practising Buddhist you may have to turn your back on Buddhism for a while in order to reach the true level. It might be that as a Christian you may have to turn your back on Christianity in order to unite with the Christ-energy, free of all dogma. Maybe the seeker within both Islam and Judaism will have to look past religion in order to get to know the true power behind Allah and Elohim? Yes, maybe we have to be ready to deny every fundamentalist idea about God and the divine in order to be able to recognize the basic energy as purely as possible?'

All of his personality radiated openness and compassion.

'Imagine that there is no more power. No limitations. You have all thought forms inside of you, everything, all. You are not a static organism. The prerequisite for seeing is that you do not cling to anything. That you understand, that everything moves. There are no final answers. There are two ways to live – consciously or unconsciously. Most people live on an unconscious level. Stagnated robots, living dead who may be able to uphold a career and support a family, but who basically may be compared to zombies without a choice. Being consciously present means to open your eyes and to see. The moment you start focusing your attention on the right place, the energies will be with you. They need you. They need your thought forms. You become a conscious servant. You say: "I am present and I am available." This is the first step towards healing. This is how you communicate with the universe. Pure thought forms. Do you see?'

He raised his hand and drew a horizontal figure eight in the air. He then kept on moving one finger in a circle until a luminous, electric current appeared. It was breathtaking. It moved.

'You see. The reaction. The pictures. Do you think all this comes from nowhere? The universe must have access to man, and that is what questions are – access. You will be recognized by them. It is a kind of cosmic, genetic material. It is totally uncomplicated. See – do you see it?'

He drew a line of pulsating light through the air.

'Movement, movement, movement. See how simple it is, how beautiful it gets.'

It was quite incredible. I could feel the same kind of ease that I had felt on Montségur, and I understood that it was possible to suspend gravity.

'Everything is so simple. The stars, the galaxies. They consist of the same minerals as we do. The same basic elements. They are our family. Ask them anything. But not: Help me, help me! That is the imperative, that doesn't work. See the beauty in taking the opposite direction. Here I am. I'm available. Then things happen. That is freedom. There is no hocus-pocus here. As a seer and a healer you do not say, this is what it looks like, this is how it is. You offer a choice. The choice of freedom. When I treat someone from afar, I simply activate or set free the clients own forgotten knowledge of his well-being. What most people cannot decide about themselves, I help them decide. I activate the options. In this connection distances are irrelevant. It takes elegance. It is a responsibility I take upon myself. It is my task to re-establish the harmony between an unhealthy organ and the universe. A closed person is no good for anyone or for the universe. I try to transform ways of thinking, karma and the purpose of life. At that moment I must dissolve myself, that which is me, everything. I'm a traveller. An ambassador of stillness. I ask my way through 48 universes and receive the answers. This is how my consultations have been for 35 years.'

'Why do we get sick?'

'Accumulation of unresolved thought forms. Not just in a single life but through one incarnation after the other. It is not necessarily the specific bad thought in itself, but it is the sum of all the bad thoughts of the person in question, which causes the breakdown. Just as it is not the specific slice of nitrite-filled salami, which kills the person, but the sum of all nitrite-filled food which eventually makes the person ill. One-sidedness and being closed up creates diseases.'

The telephone rang. The Seer went to the office to take it. He came back half an hour later.

'It was a woman from Germany. Her husband died yesterday. She wants me to guide him to the other side. I cannot do this until tomorrow, since three days should preferably pass to allow the higher bodies to be fully liberated. It's a journey that requires preparation.'

'How is this journey?'

'Beautiful. Death is not death. It is the liberation of everything you have thought in a lifetime. That is what death is.'

'When I watched you heal the Italian ambassador from

afar, yesterday, you took light crystals from the universe, what happened?'

'The various universes contain elements of the diseases that people are confronted with during the earthly refinement process, and that is why a mirror image of the person may be seen out there. Through his journey, through his incarnations on the earthly plane, man must go through a series of sufferings, sort of cosmic children's diseases. A kind of cleansing. As I said before, I am trying to reawaken the client's dormant qualities. I use the thought forms or energies of the universe, if you like. I move into Creation. It is a very beautiful kind of energy, which is constantly moving. In this case, creation in Orion's Belt. Creation uses neutrinos which are very small amounts of energy with the strange quality that they can get into all of the body, all of the planet, get out on the other side and still contain the same amount of energy. They are the carriers of the creating energy. Since they are thought forms it is possible to stop them. Just as meditation is a kind of relaxation, then this is more of a process of becoming conscious. You don't make yourself empty in order to stay empty, but in order to get filled with the power. The kind of creation I'm talking about happens every day. It is present as a possibility every day. That is the beauty of it. Then comes the Builder. The actual thought containing all thoughts. We carry that within us. And then, finally, the Accomplisher comes into force.'

'This sounds like the Father, Son and Holy Spirit?'

He nodded.

'The Accomplisher or the Holy Spirit, the conscious, cosmic breath, is an option which is always present wherever there are living creatures. But it does not function until it is activated. That is what is activated when healing happens over a distance. All people contain and are surrounded by this quality. It is outside of time and space. But it is still present everywhere. You just have to be willing to receive it. This is what I do. I wake people up and activate them. No problem. But we must always remember that it must be preceded by ethics. Unlimited man carries in him a crystallized and pure ethic, which is movable in the sense that it is made stronger concurrent with the conquering of mental limitations. It doesn't necessarily come into force automatically, but it becomes a very clear option. Demanding a choice. A prerequisite for this is that you refrain from any thought of power. This is also the prerequisite for the unlimited. It is very important to understand this. This is valid in all circumstances, big as well as small. And the one in power is always more limited than the subjugated. Since the one who wants to control others always ends up losing control over himself. It may even be felt as a threat having to give up your mental limitations, because they are locked into place and have become habitual. It takes courage. We always carry the ethical along with us and basically we all know what is right or wrong. It lies below that which is basic; by this I mean behaviour. It is part of the essential centre. When the ethic is given up, when you turn your back on it, it is a mistake. That is when diseases occur. Diseases, thus, are a mistake. But a mistake may be corrected.'

I could feel his energy directly. I experienced once more how it had a relaxing effect, which made every atom in my body fall into place.

'In order to be able to correct errors you must practise communication as purely and as directly as possible. The records and the answers you receive may not always be what you expect, but you must remember that pure energy is neutral. It is neither good nor bad. Such ideas do not exist in this context. The usual concept of being neutral does not cover the idea here.

'Universal neutrality is an active energy however, it is not tied to emotionally charged ideas. It is neither sentimental nor religious. Each person has his records within him. Your questions are situated in micro cosmos. A copy of your records are situated in the universe. Your answers are situated in macro cosmos. Answers and questions. You are situated somewhere in between, in the middle of the bridge between the one and the other, at the point of balance between inhaling and exhaling, expansion and contraction, this is where the *'you'* is, here and now. And now. And now. Do you see it? It is an eternal movement.'

The particles of light practically danced around him. He then snapped his fingers and they disappeared as fast as they had arrived.

'The existence of cosmic genetics is as common as physical genetics. The higher you get the more sensitive it is. Do not think that creation isn't sensitive. It is. At a cosmic as well as an intellectual level. All great energies are vulnerable. This is what makes them great. It can be quite frightening when you see it. The same with people. Man must find his strength in his vulnerability. Through the acknowledgement of his vulnerability and not by projecting it out as a defence. This is the way that man may break down walls. May loosen up. Make himself sensitive, increase the speed of vibration and become a cosmic being.'

He was like an age-old lotus flower. Slowly, slowly I watched it unfolding. Majestically and filled with poetry he unfolded his vulnerability, shining in golden light, and I saw that this was a spontaneous moment from which pure joy springs. He opened his hands in a welcoming gesture: 'This is happiness. A total experience of being, a total experience of NOW! As you can see, it is not comparable to winning the lottery or getting a new car. This is something totally different. It is important to understand the difference. This is where you'll find the answer to all diseases and all healing. Happiness is a deep and much more all-embracing condition which happens when we acknowledge all our being. Realization brings certainty. And certainty is knowing that we are connected to the universe. And the universe is NOW, and NOW is happiness. Happiness is healing.'

It is impossible to describe the feelings that rushed through me. It was a completely new and free energy, a quiet sparkling power of unfathomed dimensions, perhaps the kind of creation of which he had just spoken. It filled my breathing and renewed itself every time I breathed. I started to understand, that all the things he had showed me on Montségur had only been a necessary introduction, a therapeutic prerequisite for much higher layers of consciousness. This was the time where the decisive introduction to the hidden reality was beginning. It was now that I could begin to feel the fire under me of which he had spoken, and I realized that I had to stop running away. If for no other reason, then because there were no other places to hide. I realized that there was nothing to be afraid of. That that which would be devoured by the flames was merely the remains of all that had held me locked into long worn-out patterns. I had mistaken flight for movement. He looked into the air for a long time, then he said:

'Through all your incarnations you have been present on certain conditions. You never wanted to be here. You were here without being present. You saw a mountain and you climbed it. Standing on the top and recognizing that it was artificial you said: "Was this all? This is not for me." Since then everything has been a matter of unlearning. Your economy is practically nonexistent. You do not want to sing anymore. You do not want to be here. You have given up everything and withdrawn more and more from the world. You have really entered what is called *the small death*, which is not really death, but you do not live. I know all your studies. All your books. This is now opening up. That is why we are here. We are into a third principle called: *You are!* The moment you understand this, things will happen. You are the one moving the universe. It is not the other way round. You have been brought to the bottom of the hole of existence. You were never allowed to talk about everything you brought with you, your enormous, collected knowledge, everything you knew to be true. We are now going the other way and you'll now start talking about it. That is why we met. You have found the true mountain.'

His voice brought me further and further into realization:

'Your elegance was totally out of balance that day at the Central Station. Suddenly, there was no elegance. You couldn't tear yourself away. You were afraid to travel alone. Both literally and metaphorically. But you wanted to come down here. There was no doubt. You might say that your voyage through Europe in a sense was your body's message to the universe, that in spite of all the complications, you really wanted to be here. That for the first time in your life you have a sincere wish to be present as a human being.'

He got up.

'Let's go and have lunch.'

The desert wind rushed through the town, throwing tiles and flowerpots into the almost empty street. We walked further into the old part of town and found a restaurant in a small square where the wind couldn't get in. The Seer asked for a jug of water. I couldn't help thinking about the kind of pressure he must have experienced through all his years as a healer. The responsibility he had taken upon himself for thousands of people, most of whom had found their way to him only when their doctors had given up and they had nowhere else to go.

'The time has come. The moment is here. We shall dissolve the old. Forget everything about making money for tomorrow. It doesn't matter at all. When you have expressed the thought that you are going to make money, you have already limited yourself. Forget it. That is not the way it works. That is the kind of thing you find within the New Age milieu, you know: money is chakra-energy, make your first aura-million before your neighbour and all that. Limitations. Pseudo. And every time you feel you have made some progress you feel happy, and that is fine. But if you rest for too long on your laurels, you get stuck. That doesn't work. It is not the gain that matters but the effort. Not the answer but the question. Not the prize but the deed. None of my abilities matter, since they are not ascribable to me as a person. All that matters is that one is available and willing to question everything. One may not reach new conclusions, one may not get new answers, but one will obtain a new consciousness. A more embracing consciousness. One won't get a medal for it, no prizes, no Nobel prize. It simply isn't essential. That is why we haven't developed further. Man thinks about profit even before he has done the job. Thus, the job gets all too limited. He is willing to sell a new consciousness for a conclusion, a prize cup, money, prestige, anything. It doesn't work. Existence is free-flowing. When it is limited by personal ambitions, the world gets smaller. If people would realize to what extent they are connected to everything else, they would act and build their lives quite differently. It is completely indescribable what happens when the universes come back to one and say: "Finally, someone who believes." The experience that one may do something for the universes and thus for other people. That one can move somebody. Not sentimentally, not personally. Not at all – don't think that. But really move. Everything, then, becomes unbelievably beautiful and simple. One then experiences what real intuition means. What really great things are like. It is certainly not a question of making money. Never. The great thing in a specific person's development process is who he is and what he can do, seen from a universal perspective. Those are totally different criteria for success than those we know today. This is the new kind of freedom. Give me somewhere to be and I shall move the universe. This has been my life for many years. The tough years as a healer are almost over. Now, I must start helping, out there. Meanwhile, let us see what we can make of you.'

The waiter brought us sardines and a salad. My brain was like an overloaded and enormous net, in which my thoughts were racing around. I knew from Montségur that he didn't say one superfluous word, that everything had meaning and had to be considered. I knew from several experiences in his vicinity, that he made things happen, tensions and locked thoughts loosened up, the incomprehensible suddenly became understandable, the vague became clear, obvious and transparent. He transmitted the most complicated questions without a word, while the more simple, basic rules were formed in glowing sentences, word by word, materialized into earth, fire, air and water. Thus, I slowly started comprehending some of his meaning, when he talked about the fact that we and the universe have the elements in common. But one thing was how much of everything he said I was able to understand and accept. Another was everything he only hinted at and which could only be read between the lines. This was where logic and intellect failed. That's where you had to mind your P's and Q's. Shaking his head, he showed me again and again that the greatest obstacles to understanding what he tried to tell me, was my all too good manners, my dry intellect and the arrogance which followed. Luckily, his patience with me was unlimited.

After lunch we went back to the apartment. After an hour's silence we continued with questions and answers. He kept his answers simple but left it to me to decide which topics we should consider. We ended the afternoon with a breathing exercise.

'The universe is shaped like a pyramid. The equilateral triangle is the basic matrix of everything. The universe has been expanding through this form for billions and billions of years. After, comes a short silence and then the inhalation. Exactly like breathing. Expansion and contraction, inhalation and exhalation. In connection with the discovery of further universes I experienced the importance of freedom of movement. Passing beyond the universe means being unlimited. This is the way our breathing should be. But notice the short silence between the in- and exhalation. This is the moment where all problems are solved. This is where you fuse into the NOW!'

The wind had died down outside. I was in the kitchen making one of my simple meals. The Seer went and got a bottle of Don Cesar. After dinner I was overcome by a pleasant tiredness. Frank Sinatra's Rat Pack was swinging in the background. There were no hindrances. The day had settled down and I don't know what made me ask:

'Have we met each other in another life?'

The question didn't seem in the least to take him by surprise. He was warming his glass in his hands the way you do with brandy.

'We have met at a specific level of understanding. Both of us have always been aware, that although we live here on earth there is something else we have access to. Some very pure records that, unfortunately, we have not been able to use until now. It is unbelievably beautiful, but it has also been very difficult to apply and has led us along different roads to the place we are now, to this very moment in this very living room. Access to the universal level has made us shy and somehow unsuited to be here. Lonely beings since during most of our incarnations we have not been able to transform the universal to the level of the earth. When through one life after another you have been isolated with your knowledge and your ideas, a deep loneliness will arise in you as an earthling. And this has been rather difficult for the two of us. It hasn't been very pleasant but now it seems that things have started to crystallize a bit. There is an opening. Other types of consciousness. My luck is that this time I have had the great good fortune to be allowed to use my abilities to the full. It therefore looks as if I'm approaching the end. The exit is at hand. I know what it is but it is difficult to describe. This is where you come in. Otherwise it is in the interplay with my clients that I find my language. And it doesn't get any more beautiful than that. The clients and their healing is my guarantee that I'm here and that my métier is the right one. It is the basis of my studies and my research. It stimulates me to move people. My work is constantly disproved or confirmed. When I work outside the universes and am accepted by the energies, I get permission to take them back to the earth and to use them here. To transform them. And since I can transform them into something tangible, such as healing others, they open for me on a personal level. Following all my incarnations I now know that I'm allowed to be here.'

'Who are you? Where do you come from?'

A smile crept slowly over his face and disappeared in a shadow. I thought I saw him change his character in a flash. It surprised me. Suddenly, he wasn't the one I expected him to be. Did I sense a change in his voice also?

'I'm from a time before the beginning. I transcend. It was quite a shock for me when for the first time as a seer I began to understand some of my early thought forms and saw how I had abused my power. Until I acknowledged and accepted it. Then I could move on. I was present in a room where 24 energies were also present, each with its own thought form. I was the 25th energy and possessed 2. Apparently I couldn't control them. At any rate, something went terribly wrong. But I changed that later on. That is why I'm now in the process of phasing out. I used to be power. Now I'm freedom.'

The last two sentences kept hanging in the air like two snakes intertwined. A sudden impulse made me point to the two engravings I had been looking at earlier that day. It was more than a feeling. They were a part of the invisible text that had to be seen between the lines.

'How do these two pictures relate to you?'

'When I'm reading Marcus Aurelius' *Meditations*, some very familiar thought forms appear. I found that out a few years ago. I feel very close to that thought form, and it might have been an earlier incarnation. I'm not saying that I was him, but I do have a very close knowledge of the thought form Marcus Aurelius. I can even feel it in my body. The great separation he felt. The emperor who had to wage the necessary wars in order to maintain the Roman Empire, while at the same time absorbing himself in meditation. But this is *my* experience and I shall keep this to myself.'

I pointed to the painting of the Moorish room next to the other two pictures.

'You'll know that soon enough. I want to sleep now. We have a busy day tomorrow. Goodnight.'

I couldn't sleep although I was totally exhausted. Everything he told me, all the exercises we had been through, met in a whirling tornado which kept turning around in my head until everything slowly disappeared into a soft light, which grew more and more dark. I was losing my grip. Then I let go and slipped into the reality of the dream. It was totally quiet. The Moorish room with the white figure. I do not know what made me do it. Maybe it was the narrow streak of light under the door from outside. Neither do I know how it happened, but suddenly I was at the door, opening it. The hinges creaked.

The door was heavy and slow as if it hadn't been opened for a long time. I opened it wide. The noise from outside was deafening and the sunlight blinding. A big square filled with stalls. I stepped into the scorching sun and tried to find my bearings. It was overwhelming and I almost panicked. Then I started to run.

10

Everything was quiet when I woke up. My alarm clock showed half past five. I stayed in bed and listened to the silence. Then I remembered the dream and tried to recall what had happened after I stepped into the Andalusian marketplace. What had made me run? Where did I run to?

I got out of bed and walked out on to the balcony into the no-man's-land between night and day where the gritty light made everything look as if it were made of marzipan. Through an opening between the houses I could see the misty white waves of the light-green Mediterranean Sea, silently and monotonously massaging the pale ghostlike beach. Somewhere close, a woman was singing the same note, almost chant-like, spellbindingly and manically repeating it over and over again as if she wanted to warn the still sleeping town of a destiny beyond their control, which on this specific morning had disguised itself as a tall, stooping shadow desperately floating through the streets unable to find its way home. A fire was burning in that voice. A fire, which once and for all made it clear that singing is older than language. Once again I was standing at the edge of the endlessness of memory not knowing if it was mine, if it belonged to eternity or whether it was just another Andalusian mirage twirling in the wind behind the numbing veil of oblivion. I went inside in order to participate in the first quiet lesson of the day.

The telephone rang precisely at eight a.m. The Seer was deeply concentrated. I was in the kitchen but had been told not to make breakfast, neither tea nor coffee. It was the day of fast. Only water was allowed. It looked like a tough day. He had planned on using most of the afternoon for bringing the dead German man to the other side. Before that, he insisted that there should be time for me to receive the instructions for the day. He was pale when he returned from his consultations. I was ready with the glass of saltwater that he had requested. I considered suggesting that we take the afternoon off so that he could save his strength for later, but realized that it wasn't necessary to say this aloud. He nevertheless ignored it.

'The kind of movement of the inner spheres that I'm talking about has been absent from human beings far too long. Man can be intellectual, spiritual, political, artistic, highly educated, rich or anything really. These aspects only tell you something about the degree of limitation the specific person is living under, more than it is telling you anything about who this person is. When manager this, or professor that, comes to me, and he is dying and he doesn't know where else to go, it gets very clear that these titles and these medals and all these ambitions are often part of the disease. I must then make some radical corrections. At that moment all the external and vain imaginings are seen in sharp contrast to the essential, to that which really matters, such as who this person really is at his very core. Real liberation cannot happen before such a time. But you see, not many people want to acknowledge that. They cling to the medal and to their illusory estimation of their own selves as a shipwrecked man clings to the sinking ship.'

He was watching me. The sounds from the street seemed unreal as if they belonged to another world. Then he continued:

'That is why you must know the power of thought. Thoughts do have consequences. Thoughts do create form. Considering pollution and the greenhouse effect, people forget that the flow of polluting thoughts is far greater and even more poisonous than the amount of greenhouse gas. We have surrounded ourselves with so many layers of polluting thoughts that we have created a shield, which prohibits us from communicating purely with the universe. Instead, we are getting our own old and useless thought forms thrown back at us over and over again. It is developing into an evil circle. The movement is misdirected since it corrects the degree of the negative output only, which is reflected from all the unresolved, negative thought forms that are limiting our ability to see. We must change that. An enormous amount of parallel work lies ahead of us on both the personal and the collective level. Be always vigilant as to your motives. Be always willing, quite unprejudiced, to ask yourself why you do this and why you do that. Remember that everything you do, any thought, any action, will be followed by a reaction. *You* may not see it, but rest assured that someone somewhere will, and that you eventually must face the consequences. Not many people are aware of that. That is why someone throughout a whole lifetime may act on the basis of his or her own concept of good intentions without knowing that eventually, they will create negative results. In general, people do not think very much about their actions. So here is rule number one: Be conscious about your motives. Rule number two says: Let go of any kind of power. When you let go of any ambition demanding: *I want this! This is mine!* The doors will open. You will then automatically take the next step into the true, universal flow. It really hurts to notice all the limitations that man's idea of happiness, money and prestige bring forth. It is very sad. Abundance will always be present in the universe, but what does it help if man misses his opportunities and refuses to see them? The universe is on the lookout for the thoughts of man. Here is our option. All it requires is our openness. In spite of man's sophisticated way of life he still reacts primitively, but in such a specialized way that, without realizing it, he escapes the openness that I'm talking about. He sees enemies everywhere since he is projecting his unresolved thought forms onto his surroundings. The universe is looking for friends. The universe is neutral. Pure, living, moving. It contains everything. Therefore: renounce everything that implies a demand for power. Then the universe will open up.'

He got up and nodded casually towards the painting of the Moorish room which I visited in my dream:

'I see that there is already an opening.'

He went into the kitchen to get more water.

Now I also noticed what I didn't see earlier. Something had changed. Something was missing. The woman in white was gone. I got up to have a closer look at the painting. I let my finger slide across the paint where the figure had been. I saw that the door was now ajar and that a ray of light fell on the Arabian tile floor in the foreground of the painting. I felt dizzy. Did I forget to close the door properly after me? It had just been a dream. Or? Had I lost my way and not returned yet? I sat down on the sofa before he returned from the kitchen. He smiled his familiar smile.

'You look as if you could use some water.'

He poured from a large carafe before continuing his lecture.

'The concept of God is a metaphor for the highest awareness, the highest form of energy which we are all part of. Therefore we are all gods or the children of God if you like. We are created to move others. But, of course, this depends on the fact that we are aware of our true origins and true purpose. Time is ripe to let go of our old concepts. The used-up myths. The worn-out time. Time is ripe to leave the heavy thought forms behind us in return for some much faster vibrations. This is done partly by cleansing our present thought forms and by changing the old. We originate from basic matter, we were created from the first picture, primordial matter. It is everywhere but has its origin outside the universe.'

'What does the matter consist of?'

'Consciousness. Pure consciousness. It contains unconditional, unsentimental and pure love. The energy form above all energy forms.'

'You showed me how it works, but when I try to activate the energies myself nothing happens. I do have my moments, my loopholes and all that which I can't master by myself. How do I control the process myself?'

'First of all by letting go of your wish for control. That is why I keep returning to the most basic practices and ideas. If you think that the lessons become more and more difficult, you are wrong. It is the basic work, such as everything that most people skip, which is the most difficult part because it demands more renunciation, more concentration, more patience, more courage, more strength and more humour than most people are able to muster. There are no shortcuts to paradise. There are no other solutions that are easier or more simple than these. If only people would realize that. When finally we understand this, I mean really understand, then it is the simplest thing ever. Because it is universal. Cosmic. And this is what the practices are for. Liberating the universal cosmic man from all the traumas, the neuroses, projections and all other unnecessary luggage that we are carrying with us. You are beginning to understand. That is why you are here now. When you resolve the old patterns you also resolve time. Time and space are thought forms. Time doesn't necessarily extend. It is not necessarily horizontal. And the concept of space is man's beautiful but impossible attempt to encircle and secure *something*. Imagine that there are seven levels each with seven steps, then imagine that the level of vibration rises for each step, while at the same time, time as we know it is disintegrated. The way you yourself experienced it on Montségur when we experimented with time as we passed through the Gate of Time. Try to remember how heavy you felt before we started, and how day by day you felt lighter and lighter, how your vibrations became faster and faster. This was where you experienced the disintegration of time. When you get back to your daily routine it becomes difficult to be present. But it is an act of balance that you have to learn. It is the art of being here. It can be a very hard job to stay grounded when you have started to loosen up and to let go. Time doesn't exist on the seventh level. Then, you simply *are*. Man transcended.'

We strolled along the promenade. The wind had died down. It had started to drizzle instead. We passed one depressing concrete hotel after the other. At the end of the promenade we stood for a long time looking out across the sea. Far out to sea we saw something that looked like a small ship being lifted and then disappearing into a trough of the waves just to appear again a moment later. I remembered the tale about the world traveller in a small steam-driven ship who had run out of fuel in the middle of the ocean and who had to stoke the boiler with wood from the hull of the ship. Was this traveller me, I wondered? We turned and walked toward the town. The Seer was silent and I knew that he was preparing for the task ahead. But I sensed that this moment was important, like everything else that he was a part of. We walked in the same rhythm. I sensed that I was part of a larger cycle. A common breathing forming a circle, a free area, an opening where the energies were flowing freely. Even the simple task of walking became an act of the universe. We walked and we walked. Across the town, around it and back again through unknown streets and quarters. With my inner eye I saw the world traveller in his boat, which by now had been reduced to a few planks that barely could keep him and the steam engine afloat. The dissolution of self?

We stopped in front of the bullring of the town, Plaza de Toros. I followed the Seer through the gate and the corridor into the arena. No one to be seen. Raindrops made fine, dotted patterns on the dark-yellow dirt of the arena. As if it was the most natural thing in the world he opened a small gate and walked into the arena of death.

'Come on.' he said, and started walking.

The sound of his voice echoed back from the empty auditorium. I followed. He stopped at the centre of the arena.

'If you'll just stay here, I'll leave the stage to you.'

I looked at him uncomprehendingly. I had no idea what he was talking about. He kept walking toward a gate at the other end of the arena. Something was pushing against the gate from the other side. Something which made disconcerting noises. I couldn't help smiling. I simply refused to finish the thought. Although he might be unpredictable and although with him I always had to expect the unexpected, it couldn't be this. I watched him as he pulled the chains from the iron rings holding the gate in place. He slowly pushed the gate against the balustrade. I was staring into the dark shade of the opening and thought that something was moving. I couldn't believe it. The arena disappeared around me and left me floating in a yellow room.

A huge, black and shining bull was standing in the gateway. I was about to call out to the Seer but it didn't really matter now. I couldn't see him. I was frozen to the spot. My brain worked at full speed. Automatically I was considering the odds. Would I be able to find cover behind the barrier or was this giant faster than I could imagine? Would it refrain from attacking if I stood stock-still? The situation was totally surreal. Insanely ridiculous. It defied any sound reasoning. It almost looked like a cartoon without the redeeming text, which might put the craziness into perspective. The bull took one step forward. Now I could really see how big it was. A beautiful animal, which in these circumstances and in a man's mind suddenly became a symbol of evil incarnated. Now it smelled me. I shivered. Suddenly, nothing mattered. Montségur, the Grail, the Seer and all his games. Right there, at this moment, I would have given anything to get out of there in order to save my hide. The bull lowered his head and scraped with one front leg in the gravel. I looked around for the Seer in despair, but he wasn't there. That was when it took off. I watched the wide-open and snorting nostrils, I watched the gravel spraying from his hooves as they dug down, leaving secret and momentous signs. Everything happened in slow motion. I could see every muscle on the bull's neck, tense and resilient, spreading over its broad chest where the sweat formed an armour of white foam. My scream got stuck in my throat. I closed my eyes. Then I reacted, turned my body around but far too slowly. My shoes slipped on the gravel as I wanted to take off. At that moment I heard a voice in my head wordlessly saying: 'Walk towards me. Have no fear. Walk towards me!' I opened my eyes. Thousands of years of projections came at me, thundering and snorting, with flaming eyes and lowered horns. NOW! – NOW! I took one step forward. The bull ran straight through me. I felt nothing.

I turned around in order to see where it had gone, but it had disappeared like morning dew. In the auditorium a single figure was applauding me.

'Olé.'

It was the Seer.

'Olé.'

I sank slowly down onto the arena floor. Among the dots of rain in the dirt only the Seer's and my own footprints could be seen.

We sat down under an awning at a bar across from the bullring. The Seer asked for water and salt. I could feel that he paid more attention to my reactions than usual.

'Many years ago somewhere in Italy the thought form of Yeshua came to me. He said: "Why didn't you help me?" It was so simple and pure, so free of any accusation and judgement that it made me cry. You see, I was completely aware of what he meant. It was a reminder of all my major failures over the years. It was not an accusation but more of a cleansing. At that moment I realized how I had turned my back on him then, thinking that he had to deal with this himself. Yeshua was both a superhuman and an intensified force. His energies and the thought forms were so pure that his presence alone was sufficient to make things happen. He was pure. Completely pure. Showing himself to me I could see that he knew that I had known but had still not helped him. I then understood that there is nothing wrong with Yeshua or Christ, but with the Church and Christianity. They have twisted everything. We must help him, it is not up to *him* to help us. He is carrying the pure energy. That is why. Yeshua has no message as such. He was just pure. This was his single message. He had no special abilities as such, but things happened around him *because* he was pure. He was also purely isogynic. An example to be followed. *Ecce homo*. Look – this is how man can be. Yeshua was an earthly incarnation. Christ is a universal, cosmic consciousness. Christ is a choice. Christ is man's access to earthly life, a gate of consciousness. Christ consciousness is in us all. Just like the Grail.'

He sprinkled salt into his glass of water and drank.

'Also many years ago in Switzerland I experienced the thought form of Adolf Hitler appearing. He asked to be understood. He had misunderstood his task but had performed it nevertheless. Do you remember that you describe something like that in one of your books, where you experience that Adolf Hitler comes to you in a dream asking you for help? He is just a small, orphaned boy. A victim himself. Some of that was dissolved through you. Some of the thought form was cleansed through you. We all take part in the cruelty of the world. Even when we think that we know nothing about it. We all carry a Hitler and a Yeshua in us. At one time or another each person must stop and face his own failures and cruelties. Otherwise they are just projected on. It has to stop somewhere. It has to stop where forgiveness starts. All the world's dictators, whatever their names, all the concepts that we have decided are identical with evil, just like the bull today, are simply expressions of our own projections. It doesn't make sense. It doesn't justify anything, it simply tells us about our common heritage. We all take part in the cruelties. You have taken your part upon you today. You have moved from fear to freedom.'

Walking back along the promenade we looked across the sea. The waves had settled down. The small ship was nowhere to be seen.

After our quiet hour the Seer prepared to guide the deceased through *The Shaft of the Soul*. I followed him into his office. As usual he started without any hesitation. I knew that I had to be wide awake and that my total attention was required if I should have any hope of being present through this. The Seer let one of his hands hover over his desk. I closed my eyes. Inside myself the sea was like a well-waxed floor polished by an eternal breath. The exhalation spread out and flowed into nothingness, resurrecting the corners of the world and the lines and shapes of everything. It filled the void with sounds and presence for aeons. At the end of darkness, light was born. In the beautiful void the eternal NOW. Then inhalation poured back through endless time filling space with memory and new life. A golden sea of light. The memory of the initial state. The dense sound of the universe. The harmonic principle of all notes.

A single, tall, stooping figure is waiting on the beach. It is the deceased. He is almost lost in the dense fog and seems confused and scared. A burning compassion for this person. I want to call out to him, that there is no need to be afraid, help is on its way. Then a shushing finger touches my mouth. A boat approaches through the fog. The Seer is standing upright in it. He says something to the deceased, which I cannot hear, and helps him onboard. They disappear in the fog. I then hear a new note being struck. Îkhal — Ephatah a voice chants. Îkhal — Ephatah! The voice grows clearer. I recognize the insistent sound with the same light-green colour as the sea, the same pale colour as the beach, the same prickly sensation as rain against the skin, the same spellbinding element of prayer as the woman I heard singing in the morning.

I opened my eyes. The Seer was in deep concentration. I could now hear that the voice of the singing woman came from outside. I tried to repress it and to find my way through the fog, back to the memory in the great breath, but in vain. I gave up and slipped out of the office.

Two hours later the Seer had ended his work. He was pale but clearly relieved.

'Did you come along?' he asked.

I explained what I had experienced and he nodded understandingly.

'There is progress. Your sight is clearer than the last time. I'll try to explain the process as well as it may be done in words.'

He drank the glass of saltwater, which I had prepared for him.

'It is important that the deceased is left in peace for 68 hours after dying so that the person in question has discarded all his bodily elements. Then you are ready for moving through the shaft. Before leaving I ask if there is anything unfinished, something that has not yet been realized and accepted and therefore cannot be resolved. It is not an easy process. It demands great care, empathy and poise. On the walls of *The Shaft of the Soul* you see pictures of the life, recently ended. We stop and look at the pictures that call for special attention, pictures of conflicts and trials from this incarnation. I ask if the deceased understands the pictures and is able to acknowledge the motives he acted from in the various situations. When the picture is understood I ask if the deceased is ready to let it go. Major things only are pictured in the shaft. Working our way up there are fewer pictures. There both is and isn't any sense of space in the shaft. It is very difficult to describe. You experienced this yourself at Montségur. It is a kind of picture gallery where you are turning and watching the various pictures. It is in a way holographic. When the process of acknowledgement is finished and has turned into acceptance, you rise into a fantastic, intense light just before reaching the spiritual levels. Here the Collector is waiting, a ball-like thought form, collecting everything that you didn't bring with you, everything that wasn't redeemed. When I accompany the deceased we usually deal with it on the way. The deceased and I together correct the unresolved pictures and neutralize all the obstacles. If a helper isn't present, or if people do not know what is going on in *The Shaft of the Soul* before they die, they may react to the pictures they are presented with without understanding, and do not do what is necessary before moving on. All pictures are collected in what I call the Collector. This is where one is met with a light more intense than the sun, but with a softness that enables us to see it. Here you meet the two pillars of light – guardians – about the same height as a human being. Then the voyage goes on to the spiritual levels. We do not bring the pictures there. There is no need for them. On the contrary. Later, on the way back to the level of earth we pass the Collector again, going down into another *Shaft of the Soul,* confronting the pictures which were not resolved in the former life. We bring them with us into the new incarnation, where they influence us in one way or another. If we realize this here, we may practise, in the sense that every day we may ask if there is anything we should have done which we didn't do, or if we did something that we shouldn't have done. As far as I am concerned it is a part of my daily work to look at my own pictures in order to correct and hopefully to constantly be in harmony with the universal principles and the work I'm here to perform. It is a guarantee for me to be precise in my work with other people. And there is always something that needs calibration. Everything is in eternal motion so that the pictures, which were calibrated in the morning, may need a new calibration in the evening. It is quite unbelievable how little it takes for things to tilt one way or the other. The idea that the wing of a butterfly should have an effect on the weather on the other side of the globe is thus very descriptive of my point. When we have redeemed all our pictures we have finished incarnating here on earth. The earth level is a school. We are talking about a refinement process where we must learn to be conscious co-workers in this universe, so that later we can do the same in the others.'

'Where does man originate?'

'The earth is a half-way house. Man originates in the universe. The process of evaluation is firstly and lastly about consciousness and awareness. We are on the earth right now, but we belong to primordial matter, the universal consciousness, the eternal thought form.'

The Seer went to bed early. I stood for a long time in front of the painting of the Moorish room before I turned in as well. There was no sign of the figure in white. The door was still ajar.

11

It was daylight when I woke up. The rays of the sun fell through the wide-meshed curtains and formed arabesques on the wall. Listening to the sounds outside I knew that I had slept too long. Slightly confused I got up and took a bath. The Seer had already started his consultations. When he finished we had our compulsory stand-up breakfast in the kitchen. All morning he drummed the principles of distant healing into me. It was difficult for me to concentrate and my thoughts flew here and there. This just made him intensify his teaching. It was a relief when the clock struck 12.

'You look as if you could do with a change. Let us have some lunch.'

We drove towards Marbella along *la Carretera de la Muerta*. He parked in a multi-storey car park situated near one of the many fashionable malls, where designer goods and prizes competed for the impertinence award. If material poverty existed in Marbella it was very well hidden. The only person apart from the two of us who stuck out like a sore thumb in these surroundings was a young gipsy woman in a washed-out, flowery dress walking down the main street. She was so beautiful, and moved with such grace, that everyone had to stop and turn to admire her. We continued towards Puerto Banús.

'This is where some of the richest people meet. The Spaniards call it the playground of the rich. Almost everyone here is a foreigner. The Andalusians come here only to work in the bars and the restaurants.'

An impressive marina was spread out as far as you could see. One enormous vessel next to the other. Onboard some of them were uniformed crew of North African descent busy varnishing masts, scrubbing decks or polishing brass. Red carpets covered the gilded gangways. Cars worth millions were parked side by side along the pier. Well-groomed and sun-tanned men and women in expensive fashionable clothes were having lunch outside six-star restaurants. We found a table under an awning in front of a small Moroccan bar at the outskirts of the promenade. The Seer asked for pastis and water.

'Look around. Look at all the yachts. Some of them the size of ferry boats. Look at the cars. All this represents energy. But they are locked forms of energy. They have no value in and of themselves. It is just money. A dead weight without any use. The ships are seldom out sailing. They simply stay moored at the pier as a symbol of the wealth of the owner. Just like the cars. Look at the one getting out of the Ferrari. This is the moment that matters to those who come here. We are the ones who at this moment may watch this man walk from his extremely expensive car to an even more expensive yacht, just to give a silent command to one of the uniformed crew in order to be seen by us and others here. He is not going anywhere. He is certainly not going sailing. He is only confirming his own and our insatiable need for confirmation and material security. The irony is, that on the other side of the Mediterranean on the northern coast of Africa, they really want to go sailing. So much so that they are quite satisfied even with a battered rubber dingy. Every night they come ashore along the Spanish Riviera, if they get that far, only to be sent back. It may cost them as much as their life savings. Or their lives. At the same time we are sitting here with our drinks contemplating life.'

'What are we doing to change all this?'

'Well, you can't do it just like that. We must follow the universal laws. We must let go of sentimentality and try to live up to our own dignity, or what is left of it. What we consider a social privilege and an imbalance is connected to karma. This, of course, doesn't mean that we should refrain from reacting to other people's misfortunes, since this is our dharmic challenge, considering the fact that we are well off materially. The thought forms of greed are the greatest curse of the Western world. Therefore, money must also be transformed into a universal means in order to represent real values to be used in the service of good causes. Everything may be misused. When you let go of the power of money, when you refuse to be obsessed by it, when you work in harmony with the universe, you will never lack anything. When in the beginning I charged people for my treatments, I sometimes thought that I should increase the amount, since I didn't charge very much. I thought that since people are willing to pay 3,000 for a bicycle, they should be willing to pay something to improve their health. But no. I was immediately told from above that I shouldn't do that. I only needed enough money to sustain a living. That's how it was. The moment I accepted this I never needed anything. And it has been like that ever since. This is how I understand the energy of money. This is how it works. Let all your worries about money go. Life is too short to waste on things like that. Establish your life so that you are not burdened with the dead weight of material things. Do not make yourself a slave of consumption and expensive habits. Always be ready to let go of material possessions. Everything on earth is borrowed. This way you will always be able to move and be free.'

He pushed the brim of his straw hat up with the point of his finger. We ordered grilled eggplants.

'In this way you become one with the universal pulse. In this way you may be 100 per cent present without being burdened by heavy trivialities. The beautiful *doña* in the main street a minute ago, the one that everybody turned around to see, was a good example of being present unconsciously. There was an incredible ease in her bearing, while at the same time she conquered the space and the sidewalk in a very feminine and earthly way. It was obvious, that the way she walked, the swinging of her hips, her agility, the bearing of her back and the back of her neck, was a song to the present. She was present in the moment. As soon as she was seen, everything artificial, all illusions and all the props came tumbling down. All the fashion clothes and all the expensive jewellery lost their value. Her mere presence cancelled out all that was false. It was pure art.'

The waiter served the grilled eggplants covered with a layer of minced garlic and parsley stirred in olive oil. On the side we had home-made hummus and pitta bread with fresh salad.

'When you are imprisoned by money and material slavery and feel down, it can be very difficult to imagine a way out. Instinctively you know that it involves a good deal of problems because it demands a confrontation with personal pride and the masks you hide behind. But it doesn't have to be either painful or difficult. It takes humour to be a spiritual person. Humour is elegant. It transforms and opens up. Sarcasm, however, freezes up and closes. Sarcasm is just an extension of the smallness of limited man. Humour comes from the heart. When I started out as a healer I always diagnosed the clients the day before they were to arrive. One day I had diagnosed a client as suffering from some kind of problem in the right ovary. When next morning I found out that the client was a man I nearly collapsed with laughter. When I told the client why, he also fell about laughing, and I do believe that this is the only client I have had where the problem was solved with the help of humour alone. It was a very liberating and worthwhile experience. Humour is first and foremost the ability to look at oneself in a disarming light. It takes humour to be able to go out into the universes and ask questions. And it takes elegance to be here. It's like a dance. A cosmic dance. The higher the levels the more dance and humour you need. This is how you can be present, moving and dancing.'

'What happens in this dance?'

'You leave your personality behind. Otherwise you cannot communicate through energies.'

'You are neutral then?'

'Oh, I wouldn't call it that. It is more like a state of nonpersonality.'

His warm laughter made people turn around.

'It's a fantastic feeling. It is like touching your transpersonal consciousness, looking at this consciousness while you are looking. It is indescribably beautiful and it makes me laugh every time. Sometimes I really must make an effort. I reach an edge, and I must say, OK, this is humour. I like that. At this level all the heavy stuff, all the slow stuff is resolved and you feel so relieved.'

He beamed like the sun. I could see that here was a direct line to his innermost being.

'It is deeply serious but in a light and elegant, dancing

and humorous way. Beyond all words and concepts. To move *along with* the energies. In spite of all the dark matter, which I call complementary matter, the universe is full of humour and lightness.'

I was thinking that what he had just said was similar to the words of a Christian mystic: 'I now see that the eyes through which I see God are the same eyes through which God sees me.' I understood that the isogynic condition to which the Seer had introduced me might be identical to the words of Yeshua in The Gospel of Thomas: 'When you make the two into one, and when you make the inner like the outer and the outer like the inner, and the upper like the lower, and when you make male and female into a single one, so the male will not be male and the female will not be female ... then you will enter the Kingdom.'

The Seer continued:

'You're an elegant person. You claim your right to move. In order to be able to do that, you are aware that you must phase out your personality, such as your ambitions to be someone in the musical field. All the outer stuff. If you are going to open completely and uncompromisingly to the energies, there is no room for a personality which first and foremost is tied to worldly ambition. I've also been phasing out for a long while. It really takes humour. This is how you become a cosmic dancer. That's the way it is with the writing you are going to do. You won't write for anyone or to gain anything. You will be writing a book. You won't tell people how they are but simply give them an option. Your task is to tell about the options that are available. Without setting conditions. Man – think! That's all.'

He became silent and looked at me with the long glance that I had come to know so well. He looked right through me. The galaxies rotated.

'You never belonged to anyone. Because your thoughts

were extraordinary, you didn't want to limit yourself. You have always known, through your observations which were crystal-like, that you had access to some thought forms which were extraordinary. Then the abhorrence of other people's opinions arose. Opinions that you couldn't accept. Their battle to become something special didn't interest you at all. You were used by others during the incarnations immediately preceding this one. Your abilities were exploited, until the day you stated that you didn't have any money, no dignity, nothing. Going back before the incarnations it gets a bit more vague since we are talking about some very extreme thought forms. In the first picture of you, time does not exist. You *knew*. Your sophistication then, before all the incarnations, was not of the earth. You have always been a stranger here. The refined being who didn't want to communicate. You knew then that you wouldn't be understood if you opened up your potential. Thus your loneliness increased through the incarnations. You were not allowed to tell. You have always been on the lookout for your own language. But that language has never been accepted. Nobody understood. That is why you are a cripple on this earth. You have now found your forgotten language. The language that can move. You are getting close to a state of mind where you are able to be present. Of course you have taken drugs. I would have done the same in your place. In order to get back, in order to start all over again. You have been used through all your incarnations. You were an itinerant singer here in Spain. During this incarnation you have been a singer in Denmark and have tried to be present in this way, but without success. You are too extreme. You didn't get close to a common consciousness. You are not plain. Your elegance is in your thought forms, and not very many have been able to fathom and accept those. You have never been present.'

He ordered more water and pastis.

'The new man knows what it means to be a non-personality.

This is the point when you are willing to ask the question: "Who am I not?" Assuming of course that you know who you are, and which masks you have been hiding behind at a behavioural, psychological level. True being can only come from non-being, the same way that sound can only come from silence and light from darkness. The concept of the great emptiness of nonexistence is simply an illusion, just as personality is, seen in a universal perspective. The emptiness you experience in connection with the phasing out of your personality is in reality the fullness from which all living things are created.'

He stopped talking in order to make sure that I knew what he was talking about. I nodded and he continued:

'It is both beautiful and touching when a person, for the first half of his life, fights his own battle in order to fulfil all his dreams and ambitions of being someone. But in a way it is also sad, because this battle takes him away from his real destiny. The ambitions and the dreams are in command. If they are fulfilled they simply create further, transient dreams. If they remain unfulfilled they bind the person. That is why I always recommend that young people realize or phase out the ambitions of the "I," before they get too old. Such a development is in fact a prerequisite to all that I'm talking about and all that we are working with. The most efficient way of breaking that kind of power is to say: "I am not!" This is an enormous quantum leap. Imagine the freedom when you are nobody and you do not want to be anybody, you are simply present, freed from all demands and illusions. Do not confuse this with escape. On the contrary, it is a higher state, a state where your consciousness is expanded, the perfect way of being present. Through my work I can see how much of the known medicine is not working anymore, and therefore I have the feeling that a new human being is on its way. The energies of man have moved somewhat. I see it in the electromagnetic fields. All the energies in the universe are moving closer. Thus, it is my opinion that basic matter will play a decisive role in the lives of the new human being, since basic matter is found both in man and in the universe. Man must also find out how to be present in a new way. He must transform the backlog of old energies and thought forms which are imprisoning him. Man is so busy *being something* in order to be able to say that he has a personality with these or those qualifications, one who has made a lot of money has done this or that. This insistence on your own space and all your illusions and the artificial jewels is static and limiting. Thus, man is reducing himself to merely a survivor, one who is clinging to life like a dead weight. Then he doesn't dance. Man must be willing to step out into the unknown and risk himself where he cannot hide behind his own prejudices and projections, but, totally clean, make himself available to the universal principle. Man is a transformer, a channel for the universal, where the energies are transformed. This is his destiny. When man understands that, he becomes free and pliant and he thus transforms himself into *one big open moment*.'

He raised his glass as a sign that the lecture was over.
'Pastis!'

Coming back to the apartment we practised an hour of silence. I sat down in the living room and tried to connect to the concentration of energies that the Seer had activated. I knew that the ability to disregard any imagination, any demand and any prejudice was the first prerequisite for it to happen. Oppenheimer once said that it was easier to split an atom than our prejudices. The Seer said that we must distinguish between the instinctive level, where we are driven by our needs and our egocentricity, and the intuitive level, where we are sympathetic and compassionate. The difference between the two levels is a question of to what degree you master your own thoughts. When the hour had passed the Seer came in with a bottle of red wine and a single glass. He must have read my thoughts as usual as he began the lesson for the afternoon:

'I have mentioned the importance of the correct use of the power of thought earlier. We shall now conduct an experiment which will show you the practice of my theory.'

He pulled the cork and poured some wine into the glass standing in front of me.

'Please taste it.'

I lifted the glass, took a sip, then nearly spat it out again – it was that sour. It tasted like straight vinegar. He smiled teasingly.

'Well, this may not be the most exquisite wine you can imagine. To tell you the truth it is a kind of cheap wine they use in the making of a type of marinade that I do not know. But put the glass down and let me see if I can do something about that.'

I did as I was told. He sat for a while piercing the glass with his long glance.

'Now taste it!'

Lifting the glass to my mouth I immediately sensed that the wine had changed its scent. I tasted it. It was soft and rounded like a vintage wine of the best quality.

It was amazing. Still, I had stopped being surprised by anything that was to do with him. Instead I just said the first thing that came into my mind:

'Water to wine, or vinegar to wine!'

'More like wine to you,' he said laughing.

'What you have witnessed here is a refinement process. As you see, it was very simple. The power of thought works. You can do this with all foodstuffs. This is how you bless a meal. By giving it energy. It is a good idea to get used to giving everything you eat the same energy as your own. This way your body gets no surprises. Then there are no toxins. Poison is also thoughts. That's the way it is. That is why it can be influenced. Instead of saying grace it is a good idea to ask the food you are about to eat to be with you. No matter what it is. You just send your thought into it and visualize a gas-blue colour. Thus you make sure that the energies harmonize with your body. The gas-blue colour belongs to the physical part. To the organs. Then follows the superior part, the spiritual part, the golden colour. These are the two colours that definitely work for the new man. The old chakra colours have lost their value. The problem is, that although we understand intellectually what is good and what is bad for us and can decide that we want to change things, centuries of influences are locked into the memory of the body, each and every cell, which may result in various diseases if we do not make the proper corrections. There are two colours which are completely safe: the gas-blue for the physical part in every chakra and the golden for the spiritual part. You can mix them or alternate between them. Then see what happens. See how the vibrations get going.'

We worked the rest of the afternoon with visualization exercises. From neutralizing acids in coffee and removing tensions in the back of the neck to sending noticeable energy to the chakras. It was incredibly simple when you took it seriously. Over and over he pointed out how important it is that you set yourself aside in order to connect 100 per cent purely with the matter or the person to whom you want to send energy.

'Fear is the basic concept which blocks pure communication. Fear arises from ignorance. The unconscious thought forms have a tendency to run amok, and then all hell breaks loose. Fear is an expression of limitation. Fear may also be a basic condition in the universal archives. But only because an individual, through his various incarnations, has not been able to dissolve this thought form. Then it grows, builds up and gets out of control. It is a widely spread disease of our time. But what is there to be afraid of? What is the worst that can happen? That you are going to die? We all have to die, it is just a matter of time. At the cosmic level it may be a matter of a build-up of energies, which haven't been dealt with. It may be energies, which need attention and help. In the cosmos there is no judgement over light and darkness. Good and evil are qualities that we give the energies. They do not express an either-or principle but they are always mutually interactive. Some thought forms may be linked to a specific basic matter belonging to certain types of star which may therefore interact with humans. We are counterparts of the stars.'

It was late before we had supper. Although I was tired it was a kind of tiredness that felt more like being relaxed. I was not at all in doubt that this was also part of the Seer's work with me. It was not strange therefore, that after supper he suggested that we should go to a jazz club.

The club was situated in an alleyway in the tourist area of the town. There were hardly any visitors because of the time of year. A single couple was sitting at the long, narrow and dimly lit bar looking deeply into each other's eyes. The bartender polished the glasses for the umpteenth time. A piano player was playing jazz standards on a grand piano on a raised platform to the rear of the room. We sat down at a table near the exit. The Seer asked for water only but paid for it as if it were alcohol. After an hour there were about 10, 15 guests in the room. The Seer smiled but said nothing. I didn't suspect any mischief. We were just listening to the music. The air in the room was getting thick with smoke. There was a lazy yet tense atmosphere. Suddenly he leaned across the table:

'Are you at all interested in being present?'

The question hovered threateningly in the air. I sensed that something was coming. If I didn't know that there was a deeper meaning behind the question it would have made me insecure, the way I had experienced it when he confronted me with similarly challenging questions at Montségur.

'Yes,' I said.

'Quite sure?'

'Yes!'

'There's a microphone on the piano. It's switched on. Why don't you go up and sing a song?'

I was more or less paralysed. He could move at the speed of lightening, materialize bulls and make them disappear again, change vinegar into wine and all kinds of things. It was fantastic but it didn't surprise me anymore. This, however, was totally outrageous. This was crossing a line, which now became embarrassingly clear. On the other side of that line was a whole life of stage fright, the fear of not being sufficiently good, the fear of competition, the fear of failure, the fear of the little I and its false understanding of itself. Everything that I had tried to repress. I had counted on him to respect the fact that this subject would never be up for discussion. I knew now, that from the moment he had made the suggestion, nothing could change the fact that in a few minutes I would rise up, go forward, take the microphone and sing for these people. I knew that this was the only way to break the curse of fear.

It was like a dream. When I got up on the stage the piano player was already playing an intro. I was nobody. Just a man who happened to pass by. I took the microphone and sang into the corridor of oblivion:

My funny Valentine, sweet comic Valentine, you make me smile with my heart. Your looks are laughable, unphotographable, yet you're my favourite work of art. Is your figure less than Greek? Is your mouth a little weak, when you open it to speak? Are you smart? Don't change a hair for me. Not if you care for me. Stay, little Valentine, stay! Each day is Valentine's day . . .

12

Each day is Valentine's day ...

I put the microphone back on the grand piano. No reaction. The guests stared at me with empty eyes. I thanked the piano player, stepped down from the stage and walked through the narrow room. The Seer was no longer at the table. I walked towards the exit, pushed the door open and stepped into the burning heat.

I stood still in order to let my eyes get used to the sharp sunlight. The smell of cinnamon and roses mixed with the dancing dust swirling in the air over the bustling marketplace. I was at the square just outside Isathar's house. The door was ajar. I spotted her in the crowd. She smiled and gave me her most confident and passionate look. I wanted to take her in my arms and make love to her there and then, but I withstood the temptation. I turned my back on her and looked at the multicoloured view in front of me instead, in order to find a place to sing. People had come from the remotest corners of the Moorish kingdom to participate in the festivity. Even the Caliph of Granada had announced his arrival. All kinds of artists were to be seen: fortune-tellers, animal trainers, female dancers, storytellers, singers, writers and calligraphers. I walked along stalls with all kinds of magnificent merchandise and commodities: beautifully woven materials from Mecca, spices from Cairo, sables and swords from Toledo, valuable things of gold and silver, beautifully bound manuscripts from Cordoba with the poetry of the prophets. Then it all fused into one. I do not remember anything else.

One day followed the next. But no two of them were alike. The further into the universe the Seer took me, the closer to the ground I got. However, it was not comparable to anything I had tried or even been close to before. It was a totally new way of being present. It opened me up to another kind of perception, a sharpened form of attention, which until now I had only experienced as holes in reality. The holes that I, on and off, had fallen through and sought shelter in. Thanks to the Seer these moments were now turning into tools that I could consciously make use of. The time was getting close where I would have to take over and bring everything he taught me into a new world. The teaching about the isogynic human being. But there was still something indefinable just below the surface. A memory. Something which for a long time had been in hiding behind an impenetrable veil, but which was now unveiling and becoming visible in dreams and visions. An infinite number of small streams uniting into a river, which moved slowly toward the open sea.

I woke up early one morning and was sitting on the terrace. It had just stopped raining and the air was fresh and clean. I was just sitting there being present, when I noticed a raindrop hanging from the edge of a folded sunshade, shining like a diamond in the growing morning light. Getting close to it I noticed that it was reflecting everything around it, 180 degrees. Looking into the raindrop I could see the wealth of microscopic life in it. It was a whole universe in itself, while at the same time it was connected to the larger universe it was reflecting. In a little while when the time was ripe it would fall and mix with the water forming a small pool at the foot of the sunshade. At that moment the drop of rain would stop being a drop. But it would still exist as water. During the day the sun would cause the water to evaporate and form a small cloud. Tonight the cloud would dissolve and fall like dew or like rain. And tomorrow morning I might once more be watching a drop on the edge of the Seer's sunshade. This was the working of the simple law of the disappearance and reappearance of everything that is. The cosmic cycle. *Gravity and grace.*

The clouds above me were opening up. The clouds which I knew contained the rain of memory. A drop here and drop there. The river was growing and becoming more and more majestic.

Indeed, he had met a stranger. He was right about that. But never in his life had he met anyone like this stranger. He had never heard anyone speaking in such simple and understandable terms about inconceivable things. The words that came out of this man's mouth tugged at his heartstrings. Right where the blood was dripping with all the new and incomprehensible things which had been so decisive, but which also in some inscrutable way had also brought him hope about another kind of life, hope that he might break through the fatal horizon. The words of this man had brought him to a state of tranquillity which he hadn't known since his earliest childhood. Like a mother breast-feeding her child, after which the child falls asleep in her arms, full and tired.

'Perfect!' the man had said — 'just perfect!'

He didn't remember for how long he had stayed in this small community but it had been a staggering experience. He didn't understand. But he could feel it.

People who wanted to help. Generous people. People with no other weapons than the words they had at their disposal. He didn't understand them, but he felt them, and shortly after, the pains in his chest had disappeared as suddenly as they had come.

But the day came when he had to move on, and they told him about the paradise he was looking for and that he might be able to find it among the Moors at Alhambra, but that the paradise he was really looking for would always be within his reach and that he didn't have to travel to get to it. But, since this was the way it seemed to be, they would have to let him go and they told him in what direction he should go. He then left the Pyrenees and travelled to the land of Spain.

This is what I wrote in one of my books three years before an angel sent me into the arms of the Seer. And there was more. Much more. I began to see that a major part of what I had written was not just about things that had happened, but also very much about things that were to come. I then remembered the Seer telling me that it was a matter of being it and writing it, furthermore he had suggested that by accessing the memory I had to reinvent my forgotten language and I had to learn to see. I had to find a way of being present. A way back to life. This left only one last question. If life was the paper and man the pen, whose hand then was to take the pen and do the writing?

One day when the Seer and I were walking along the promenade, we continued our walk past the last of the hotels and building sites with only partly finished *appartementos* and into the poor part of the town, which more or less looked like a suburb. Washing was hanging from clothes-lines across the streets. A couple of prostitutes were offering their services at a street corner. Dogs roamed freely, and behind the houses cockroaches the size of mice were scurrying in and out of the garbage piles. The sweet smell of rat poison mixed with the unmistakable stench from the overloaded sewer system. The houses moaned with euro disco and fandango. The sunlight was broken by a forest of TV aerials and satellite dishes and made the shadows flicker and dance a grotesque fandango in the narrow streets. We had walked for a while without talking. I had the feeling of walking next to myself – further and further into an unreal state of mind.

A dark-skinned man crossed the street and disappeared into a small bar. I could hear Arabian music. The atmosphere of a repressed life within this maze-like quarter of the town somehow resembled the blacked-out maze of my memory.

'This is the place in your memory you keep returning to without understanding or seeing the connection.'

I didn't understand what he was talking about.

'What does this mean?'

We stepped into an old square filled with shaky tables and stalls. The sun was scorching. I squinted in order to see better. For a moment I thought I saw people dressed in foreign clothes, women in veils and flowing oriental robes, men in capes and turbans. The Seer walked into the throng of people. I followed. He stopped in the middle of the square.

'Take note of this place,' he said.

The sun hung right above us. At the same moment, out of the corner of my eye, I saw the man from before coming out of the Arabian bar.

The Seer saw right through me. The black galaxies were turning through the universe. His voice was quite clear. But still, it felt as if he was talking to me from another era.

'We have stood here before, you and I.'

The sentence echoed through the endless corridors of my

memory. *We have stood here before, you and I — we have stood here before, you and I.* Something made me turn my head toward the bar. The rays of the sun reflected in a shining object and blinded me. I could just glimpse a dark figure standing outside.

'I have been waiting for this moment for a long time.'

The voice ricocheted off the walls of the corridor. *This moment — this moment — this moment — this moment!* I had my doubts at first. But then I saw that it was true. The dark man was watching us. My eyes met his for a fraction of a second. In this fraction of a second I looked into a burning desert of stars and loneliness. Looked into ... It was impossible. It couldn't be. Slowly he began moving towards us. I was about to signal to him when the Seer took my arm. Everything stood still. Like a held breath. Like a raindrop suspended in mid-air before disappearing into the sea. Then the man turned around and ran back towards the bar. He almost overturned a jewellery stall before disappearing through the door he had emerged from a little earlier. A young gypsy woman shouted after him. I wanted to say something but the words stuck in my throat. Then I lost sight of her. The Seer was quietly watching me. Everything happened so fast. Life continued around us. Then he pointed to a stall where a man was selling antique haberdashery and old bits and pieces, and said as if nothing had happened:

'I'm almost certain that this metal box contains something belonging to me.'

We walked over to the stall. The man opened the metal box and took out an old silver coin and gave it to the Seer. They negotiated for a while. The Seer paid him. A little later he handed me the coin. On it was the image of a man crowned with laurels, a Roman. I could hardly believe my eyes. It was Marcus Aurelius.

'It looks as if everything is going to join here and now. It seems as if those up there are speaking quite loudly – and at the same time. And you really look as if you could do with a pastis.'

I was still shaken when we returned to the apartment. On the wall of the living room, next to the old engraving of the emperor Aurelius, was the picture of the Moorish room. The woman dressed in white was still nowhere to be seen. Had she ever existed? Or was she Zoé the isogynic one, Prat the guardian of nature, Isathar the gypsy or the incarnation of all three? The mother, the earth mother, the maiden. The incarnation of the feminine principle. The Norns – Urd, Verdante, Skuld? The isogynic duplicate in every human being?

The Seer placed a carafe of water on the table.

'The sexes find each other in their hidden half. A relationship between man and woman must first and foremost work as a mirror, in which both parts mutually integrate with each other, thus getting close to the isogynic state. Seen from a universal point of view, man has unfortunately reduced the relationship to a playground game called mum, dad and children. There are much more powerful forces at stake. If you look at the chakras, man is still stuck at the second chakra connected with sexuality. But according to the evolution and the cosmic laws, man should really be at the thought form of the third chakra. We are still stuck in the remains of the previous millennia. That is why sexuality goes berserk, so that man cannot control the sexual energy but ends up letting it control him. The result is that too much egotism is expressed and this is pulling in the wrong direction. Man has turned sexuality into a party game to fight off boredom. Our culture has worn out the concept of love. It is eradicated daily by the media, in commercials, songs, novels, movies and anywhere one can get away with it. Love doesn't get deeper just because it speaks with big, pink, lisping letters, does it now? Since we are so focused on this, more and more unclean thought forms are produced, binding man instead of setting him free. Probably because it is so easy to lose yourself in sexuality. But losing oneself is not the same as transforming oneself. And this is the purpose of the union between woman and man.'

I then turn around to look for Isathar but I cannot see her. At one of the stalls I spot a manuscript so beautifully made that I linger for a while admiring it. As I'm about to pick it up I am overwhelmed by a strong feeling. An inexplicable certainty makes me leave it where it is and walk on. Driven by unknown forces I'm moved along by the throng of people into a state of mind which suddenly changes everything. Two men are talking to each other at a distance from me. It is as if my reality is torn apart. I am rooted to the spot. I have a feeling that I know them but I don't know from where. Now, one of them turns and spots me. His eyes shine like the sun and burn with fire. He is pointing at me. Are they men of the Inquisition? I feel panic spreading in me. I have no intention of waiting to find out who they are. I start running. Back to Isathar's house. I see nothing. Bump into everything. I hear a voice calling out my name. Isathar's voice? I cannot even calm down when I'm in Isathar's cool room with the door closed behind me. My heart is beating like mad. A sound at the door. A shadow in the opening. Isathar, Thank God. She looks at me, surprised.

'What happened?'

'Nothing,' I said.

I don't want to talk about it. I want to forget everything. Maybe it is really just my own senses playing a trick on me? She doesn't look convinced. I walk over and hold her. She puts her arms around my neck. Slowly I loosen the hidden strings in the top of her white dress. She smiles in the darkness and lets me do what I want. I kiss her on the mouth. It is not easy to undress a woman. I touch her breasts lightly. Let my hands

*slide down along her back. Then she is standing in front of me
as God created her. Shining. Vibrant. I let my cape fall to the
floor and we both slide down together. I hold her close, I kiss her
and sense her secretive scent of cinnamon. How could I ever
forget that? How could I forget this creature opening herself so
generously like a rose in bloom? I bow down and break the seal
of the rose. Slowly we ride through a primitive land, heavy and
bursting, towards distant horizons. Later the landscape opens
up. It is summer and we are travelling through endless, foreign
lands. I see a boy and a girl bathing in a stream. See the boy
following the girl toward a lake. See them merge into each other,
becoming one. See them lying side by side after growing old.
Smiling, very much aware that they are about to die. I look
into the burning eyes of Isathar. She dissolves all my mistakes
and all my deceits. I see the black galaxies glimmering. I arm
the bow of the blue moon with the golden arrow of the sun. I
let go and let myself fall. I fall freely and eternally through
her timeless universe. To the secret of pain and light in her
innermost being ... Zoé, Prat, Isathar.*

Sophia — Hokhmah.

*Nehwey sibyanak aykana d'shmaya aph b'arah. Let that
happen on earth, which is written in between the stars. Unfold
the light of the universe through us in harmony with universal
laws. Never again shall anything keep us apart. From this
moment on I shall always be free.*

A few days later the Seer drove me to the railway station in
Malaga. Waiting on the platform, he gave me a parcel. It was
relatively heavy.

'This may be the answer to the questions you have been
asking yourself for a long time.'

The words were burning in the air. I knew that he saw
me the way I am. I, on the other hand, saw the galaxies in his
eyes floating quietly through the universes, hovering on the

Zoé, Prat, Isathar
What is hidden must be unveiled

breath of timelessness. A memory disappearing in a grand, open moment. Liberated from any kind of limitation. He left without saying good-bye and without looking back. Elegant as always, dancingly present, moving everything. I had a lump in my throat and a tear in the corner of my eye. If he had seen this he would jokingly have told me that I was sentimental. I leaned out of the window of the compartment and saw him disappearing in the throng of people. A stream in a flood. A drop in the ocean.

The train lurched forward with a jerk. I opened the parcel. It contained a manuscript almost 400 pages long. The main title was, 'Kansbar, the Protector of the Grail'.

And below, 'Alhambra 1001'. Then a small introduction. I started to read:

'Kansbar is not my real name. But due to the secrets I have been chosen to guard, I have taken this old, Persian name. Kansbar the Chosen One. Kansbar the Wise. Kansbar the Seer. Kansbar, the Protector of the Grail. I am getting old. For many years I have been searching for the one who is to take over this duty after me. But in vain. Not until now do I remember the day I met Flegetanis, an itinerant Moorish singer, at a marketplace in a small town on the coast of Andalusia. This manuscript is for him. This is the story of the Grail.'

I put the manuscript down. A slight electric current ran up my spine. It felt like a fine tension slowly spreading its energy all through my body. I just saw the sun setting behind the mountains before the train roared into the endless tunnel of memory. *Rukha d'koodsha — malkoota d'shmaya, Rukha d'koodsha — malkoota d'shmaya, Rukha d'koodsha — malkoota d'shmaya.*